YANKEE STONECUTTERS

LAFAYETTE VIEWING CANOVA'S STATUE OF WASHINGTON IN THE OLD STATE HOUSE, RALEIGH, NORTH CAROLINA

YANKEE STONECUTTERS

The First American School of Sculpture
1800-1850

By Albert TenEyck Gardner

Essay Index Reprint Series

BOOKS FOR LIBRARIES PRESS
FREEPORT, NEW YORK

LIBRARY OF CONGRESS CATALOG CARD NUMBER:
68-58790

PRINTED IN THE UNITED STATES OF AMERICA

INTRODUCTORY NOTE

The original purpose of this book was to provide a catalogue of the collection of early-nineteenth-century American sculpture in the Metropolitan Museum of Art. As the compilation of material for the catalogue went forward, so many interesting facts came to light which explained the curiosities of the rise of the First American School of Sculpture that it was decided to embody them in a series of informal essays. These attempt to place the sculptors and their works in relation to the life of the time. It has been the aim throughout this book to treat the subject as a part of the larger pattern of American life rather than to isolate it in a separate history of sculpture — an art too often considered as something quite divorced from life in general.

Judged solely as works of art, the productions of the entire school have perhaps only a moderate significance. The principal importance of these sculptors' lives and works to us today would seem to be their great value as social, cultural, and historical documents. It is not the purpose of this book to endeavor to renew the dessicated crowns of laurel so relentlessly pressed upon the sculptors' untroubled brows by their impetuous and well-meaning contemporaries.

In consideration of this point of view, the main body of the text has been arranged upon the following pattern: first, two chapters on certain phases of the patronage of sculptors; second, two chapters on the artists themselves, as a group and as individuals; finally, an examination of the two dominant influences of the time —romance and machines—as they affected the lives and works of the sculptors. The catalogue of the sculpture in the Museum, reduced to a list, will be found in the Appendix. Following the text is a biographical dictionary of more than a hundred American sculptors both native and immigrant, born between 1800 and 1830, who grew to maturity before the Civil War and constitute the First American School of Sculpture.

The author wishes especially to express his indebtedness to Horace H. F. Jayne, Vice Director of the Metropolitan Museum of Art, for his continued interest and encouragement as well as for many valued suggestions which have been incorporated in this book.

The author makes grateful acknowledgement to the following publishers for permission to quote from the works cited: to E. P. Dutton, Van Wyck Brooks' *The Flowering of New England;* to Harper and Brothers, Mark Twain's *Innocents Abroad;* to Houghton Mifflin Company, Emerson's *Journals* and Henry James' *William Wetmore Story and His Friends;* to Little, Brown and Company, *The Letters of Mrs. Henry Adams,* edited by Ward Thoron; to Random House, Emerson's *Complete Essays,* edited by Brooks Atkinson (Modern Library Edition); to Charles Scribners Sons, Maitland Armstrong's *Day Before Yesterday;* to Yale University Press, *The Correspondence of James Fenimore Cooper.* Thanks are also due the North Carolina Historical Commission for permission to quote R. D. W. Conner's *Canova's Statue of Washington.*

A. T. G.

The Metropolitan Museum of Art
New York
December, 1944

TABLE OF CONTENTS

Part I: The Ingenious Yankee Mechanic

Part II: The First American School of Sculpture

LIST OF PLATES

Frontispiece

THE MARQUISE DE LAFAYETTE VIEWING THE STATUE OF GEORGE WASHINGTON BY ANTONIO CANOVA IN THE OLD STATE HOUSE, RALEIGH, NORTH CAROLINA (1825)
Lithograph, from a painting by J. Weisman and Emmanuel Leutze (1840). Collection of the North Carolina State Department of Archives and History, Raleigh, N. C.

I

Fig. 1. THE STATUARY ROOM OF THE ATHENAEUM, BOSTON (1850–1860)
Woodcut, Collection of the Author

Fig. 2. THE STUDIO OF HIRAM POWERS, FLORENCE, ITALY (1850–1860)
Woodcut, Collection of the Author

II

Fig. 1. HIRAM POWERS' *GREEK SLAVE* ON EXHIBITION IN THE DÜSSELDORF GALLERY, NEW YORK (1857)
Engraving, Collection of the Author

Fig. 2. A PARTY OF TOURISTS INSPECTING THE SCULPTURE IN THE GALLERIES OF THE VATICAN BY TORCHLIGHT, ROME (1858)
Woodcut, Collection of the Author

Fig. 3. ITALIAN IMAGE-MAKERS, NEW YORK CITY (1850–1860)
Woodcut, Collection of the Author

III

GEORGE WASHINGTON, BY HORATIO GREENOUGH
Marble, Florence (1832–1843), Collection of the Smithsonian Institution, Washington, D. C.
(Originally designed for the center of the Rotunda of the Capitol)

IV

ANDREW JACKSON, BY HIRAM POWERS
Marble, Florence (1836–1837); height 34¼ inches. Collection of the Metropolitan Museum of Art, New York
(Photograph, Charles Sheeler)

V

Fig. 1. THE GENIUS OF MIRTH, BY THOMAS CRAWFORD
Marble, Rome (1843); height 46 inches. Collection of the Metropolitan Museum of Art, New York

Fig. 2. THE WHITE CAPTIVE, BY ERASTUS DOW PALMER
Marble, Albany, N. Y. (1859); height 66 inches. Collection of the Metropolitan Museum of Art, New York

VI

Fig. 1. ARMED FREEDOM, BY THOMAS CRAWFORD
Plaster, Rome; colossal. Collection of the Smithsonian Institution, Washington, D. C.
(A bronze cast of this surmounts the dome of the Capitol)

Fig. 2. "WOUNDED TO THE REAR," ONE MORE SHOT, BY JOHN ROGERS
Bronze, New York (1865); height 23 inches. Collection of the Metropolitan Museum of Art, New York

VII

Fig. 1. WASHINGTON ALLSTON, BY EDWARD AUGUSTUS BRACKETT

Marble, Boston (1844); height 26¾ inches. Collection of the Metropolitan Museum of Art, New York

Fig. 2. HENRY CLAY, BY SHOBAL VAIL CLEVENGER

Marble, Florence (1842); height 30¼ inches. Collection of the Metropolitan Museum of Art, New York

VIII

Fig. 1. CLEOPATRA, BY WILLIAM WETMORE STORY

Marble, Rome (1858); height 54½ inches (this example a replica, 1869). Collection of the
Metropolitan Museum of Art, New York

Fig. 2. LATONA AND HER CHILDREN, APOLLO AND DIANA
BY WILLIAM HENRY RINEHART

Marble, Rome (1873–1874); height 46 inches. Collection of the Metropolitan Museum of Art, New York

IX

THE DYING CENTAUR, BY WILLIAM RIMMER

Bronze (c. 1870); height 21½ inches. Collection of the Metropolitan Museum of Art, New York

X

THE FIGHTING LIONS, BY WILLIAM RIMMER

Bronze (c. 1870); height 16½ inches. Collection of the Metropolitan Museum of Art, New York

XI

THE FALLING GLADIATOR, BY WILLIAM RIMMER

Bronze (c. 1861); height 62¾ inches. Collection of the Metropolitan Museum of Art, New York

XII

Fig. 1. ANDREW JACKSON MONUMENT, BY CLARK MILLS

Bronze, Washington (1853). Lafayette Square, Washington, D.C.

Fig. 2. VIEW IN THE SCULPTURE GALLERY, METROPOLITAN MUSEUM OF ART,
NEW YORK (1890–1900)

PART I

The Ingenious Yankee Mechanic

I · NATIONAL MONUMENT
or, Sculpture and Politics

"Sculptor! thy hand hath moulded into form
  The haggard features of a time-worn face;
  And whosoever views thy work shall trace
  An age of sorrow, and a life of storm!
  And canst thou model the heart? For that is warm,
  Glowing with tenderness for all its race;
  Instinct with all the sympathies that grace
  Those pure and artless bosoms where they swarm!
  Artist! May fortune smile upon thy hand!
  Go forth, and rival Greece's art sublime;
  Return, and bid the statesmen of thy land
  Live in thy marble through all after-time!
  O, snatch from heaven the fire Prometheus stole,
  And give the sculptured block a living soul!"
  JOHN QUINCY ADAMS, "To Hiram Powers"

THE American school of sculpture seems to have sprung full panoplied upon the scene in the brief space of about twenty years. This is perhaps the most striking feature of American sculpture in the nineteenth century, the sudden appearance of a group of sculptors from the restless American frontier between 1800 and 1850. Scarcely any other occupation, it would seem, could be found that would be more unlikely and exotic at such a time and in such surroundings. From the histories of American sculpture one would gather that for no apparent reason young men were suddenly seized with an irrepressible yearning to become sculptors. Perhaps such a romantic desire in the bosoms of callow farm boys and ingenious apprentices did exist, but it seems incredible that, without the aid of a more powerful and concrete stimulus, such a desire should have arisen in so many men at about the same time and that their careers should run in such a constant pattern. May it not be that this frontier phenomenon has a more simple and direct explanation? To state the fact that scores of sculptors emerged in the American social structure in twenty years would seem to presuppose that there was a *demand* for sculpture.

In 1816 it was taken for granted that no worthy native American sculptor could be found to execute a statue of George Washington for the state of North Carolina—in 1836 three young American sculptors, Horatio Greenough, Thomas Crawford, and Hiram Powers, were busy in Italy setting up studios and carving for themselves the most exalted international reputations, while at home other men were at work preparing to follow. In the next decade the magnet of Rome drew, every year, new recruits to join this little band of plastic pioneers.

What happened between 1816 and 1836 that suddenly caused backwoodsmen in Kentucky and Ohio, Connecticut Yankee farmers' sons, Irish immigrant boys in New York, and even Harvard graduates, to take up mallet and chisel? What made them fly eastward to romantic Italy when almost everyone else in the United States was heading West? Why did they exchange the prairie freedom of a Jacksonian democracy for the artificial conventions of the classic style of sculpture amid the political corruption of Italy? A survey of art histories dealing with the period gives scarcely any direct information on these interesting questions. The art historians in dealing with American sculpture seem so concerned with the luxuriant progress of the nation after the Civil War they have little time to investigate what went before, save for a bare record of lives and works. To them the sculpture of the nation evolves slowly through the century from artistic immaturity to a dazzling Beaux-Arts florescence at the World's Columbian Exposition in Chicago in 1893. The early sculptors were merely predecessors, dim precursors of the post-Civil War "giants." It seems to be taken as a matter of course that in practically no time at all a whole school of sculptors should arise out of a wilderness. It seems of only perfunctory interest that in fifteen years a smart Yankee boy like Hiram Powers could transform himself from a backwoods yokel into a world-famous rival of Praxiteles.

Our early nineteenth-century sculptors' lives and works present few other problems. Their dates are known, their works are catalogued, photographed, and forgotten. Scarcely any of their sculptured works seem to have been lost, or to have earned that special interest which is accorded to works of art that have been destroyed. Nathaniel Hawthorne's suggestion that much of the sculpture of his time would be found suitable for future generations to build into walls or burn into lime has not yet been followed.

The relation between sculpture and politics may at

first glance seem somewhat tenuous, but in the early days of the Republic the connection was obvious to everyone. Perhaps no class of men were more acutely aware of the political significance of sculpture—that is, sculpture in the classic style—than the legal and political minds of the time. To them the idea of political liberty was the most treasured heritage from classic antiquity. It was a commonplace of the day that liberty in the ancient republics of Greece and Rome was accompanied by a flourishing of the arts, notably the art of sculpture. Of course they drew the obvious parallel—if the republics of Greece produced the greatest sculpture the world had ever seen, the artists of the New World, living in a new and more perfect democracy, could not fail at least to equal the ancients in sculpture. The general feeling regarding sculpture finds expression in the words of Walter Savage Landor, who wrote "Sculpture awaits but the dawn of Freedom to rise up before new worshippers in the fullness of her glory." Again, in a letter to Emerson he says, "Sculpture at the present day [1856] flourishes more than it ever did since the days of Pericles; and America is not cast into the shadow by Europe."

In America the great victories of the Revolution and the War of 1812 had brought forth the symbolic heroes and a unity of national sentiment and pride which aroused a demand for national monuments and memorials—a demand sanctioned by classic example. The national heroes had arisen and performed their several missions. Almost before these great men had time to recline upon their bright laurels, the People—idol of heroes—demanded memorial effigies upon which to whet their patriotic or partisan enthusiasms. For a time Americans had been gratified by images in wax displayed in taverns, but these were found to be perishable and somewhat undignified. The desire for statues was, in the main, the result of normal hero worship among simple and honest men. Hundreds of Fourth of July orators linking national heroes and classic liberty gave wide circulation to the ideas that were to assist in the formation of the classico-Jacksonian school by turning Yankee talents to sculpture. Given heroes, public monuments became a national necessity. How easily pleased our forefathers were may be gauged by some of the monuments then raised and by the fabulous prices they seemed willing to pay for them. However, the point of these monuments was homage to heroes—who could stop to count the cost or to criticize?

The sublime figure of George Washington looms large upon the scene. As a national hero and as an abstract symbol of liberty and national unity, he was the rallying point—the serene center—about which all Americans united. His dignity and virtue stilled all partisan clamor. Washington the symbol may be considered as the most important single factor in the encouragement of the sculptural arts in the young nation. To him we attribute a special significance as the Father of American Sculpture. In the words of Charles Sumner, a sculptured portrait of Washington is "the highest work with which an American artist can occupy himself."[1] It is interesting to note how often merely the sight of a plaster bust of Washington by Houdon or Cerracchi determined the choice of a career in sculpture for the men of our neoclassic school.

In addition to the heroes there was the national Capitol in Washington City, as it was then called, and there were, rising, other public edifices that had to be decorated in an appropriate classical manner to satisfy the Greco-Roman republicans of the New World. Congress proved anxious to do itself honor (after a certain amount of prodding) by patronizing the arts. The legislators, if sometimes obtuse and unsure of themselves in matters of art, were most generous. After being properly primed, they handed out some extraordinary sums for sculpture that has, since its erection, remained among the greatest of national curios.

As early as 1817 the erection of an "American Repository" for the sculptured and painted portraits of Presidents and military heroes had been proposed. The idea, however, was abandoned since it was thought more important to complete the building of the national Capitol. That building seemed so vast that one critic of the proposal said, "We would much prefer to see the Capitol finished, where it is presumed ample room will be found for all the marble busts that will be made in this country for half a century to come."[2]

It might be truthfully said that the controversies attendant upon the rebuilding of the Capitol after the War of 1812 first brought the problem of sculpture forcibly to

[1] E. L. Pierce, *Memoir and Letters of Charles Sumner* (1878).
[2] C. E. Fairman, *Art and Artists of the Capitol* (1927), quoting the Washington *National Register*, Oct. 4, 1817.

the attention of the general public. Finally, the fire that consumed the State House in Raleigh, North Carolina, in 1831, again drew attention to the glaring and intolerable fact that American patriots, even at that late date, depended on Italians and other foreigners for the sculptured emblems of our national glory. One of the main forces in creating an American school of sculpture was apparently the wounded national pride. It irked statesmen and public alike to import foreign artisans from the decayed and enslaved shores of Italy to carve decorations for the Capitol of a free nation. It was scandalous that so many good American dollars had to be voted into the pockets of French and Italian sculptors when the sovereign states wished to erect memorials to the immortal heroes of the Revolution.

Where were the men who were to answer this call for native sculptors? Hiram Powers was working obscurely in the Western Museum in Cincinnati making waxworks; Horatio Greenough was studying in Europe; most of the rest of the sculptors were still boys—farmers or apprentices at one trade or another. Ten years after the fire at Raleigh there were little colonies of young American sculptors established in Italy—some in Rome with Thomas Crawford, others in Florence with Hiram Powers and Horatio Greenough. Twenty years later, in 1851, Hiram Powers, the great American sculptor from Cincinnati, was world-famed, the acknowledged heir to the classic laurel crown of Canova.

At the beginning of the century all that was considered grand and sublime in the world of art was crystalized in the sculpture of Antonio Canova. In the estimation of men of taste he had in truth revived the ancient splendors of Greek and Roman sculpture. To the learned, Canova seemed more Greek than the Greeks. He was the darling of Rome, his fame was on every tongue. With the characteristic independence of artists, he had refused the Emperor Napoleon's command invitation to come to Paris. Honors were showered upon him by kings and queens, Pope Pius VII created him Marquis and Count Palatine. The highborn Roman ladies worshipped him. His eminence and personal beauty endeared him most especially to Pauline Buonaparte, the Princess Borghese, whom he portrayed in the classic role of Venus Victrix, reclining nude upon a couch.

However, all the honors and riches that were cast before him never changed his simple manner of living, and at his death in 1822 he left all his priceless original casts and an ample estate to his native town of Possagno to form the Museo Canova. In this, and in the princely legends that grew about his name, the young American sculptors who journeyed to Italy found countless romantic and practical precedents established by him for them to aspire to. They set themselves the task of reproducing in their lives a reasonable facsimile of the success story of Canova's rise from humble beginnings to world eminence. The man, no less than his white marble gods, was for them the classic model.

Among the works of Canova his statue of Washington holds no very distinguished position. It was executed for the state of North Carolina between 1817 and 1821 at the end of his career. In the first place the face was copied from an execrable plaster bust by Cerracchi. Even at the time it was made, the most charitable critics said it was no true portrait of the General though it was admitted to be, unquestionably, a properly dignified and classical image, suitable in every way for memorializing a national hero. Washington was represented in heroic size, seated, dressed in elaborate Roman armour. At his knee he held a tablet on which he was in the act of inscribing a message to the people of the United States (written in impeccable Italian), the inscription read "Giorgio Washington al popolo degli Stati Uniti; Amici e Concittadini . . ."

After many months of slow transit from Rome the statue was finally installed and unveiled with due ceremony in the little rotunda of the State House at Raleigh on December 24, 1821. Here, in a little backwoods town of about two thousand souls, was situated the greatest work of art in the whole United States. The State House was transformed by its presence into a national shrine. The citizens of Raleigh saw immediately that something would have to be done about the condition of the building. It was a dingy, characterless brick structure, serviceable perhaps, but quite innocent of architectural adornment—utterly unworthy to house the glistening marble treasure.

The General Assembly rose to the occasion and appointed a state architect, William Nichols, a gentleman who knew the five orders and was familiar with the superb architectural monuments of antiquity. Work was begun forthwith; the grimy brick walls were sheathed with white stucco, elegant pillared porticoes were applied to the east and west facades, and the inevitable dome was raised. Rhody Atkins, the original builder, would scarcely have recognized his handiwork—the building had become a model of Federal architecture.

For almost ten years the people of Raleigh enjoyed and gloried in the beautiful statue—the state's proudest possession. Travelers frequently went out of their way to visit the town in order to see this remarkable production from the hand of the world's greatest sculptor and to pay homage to the immortal Washington. The Marquis de Lafayette had paused in Raleigh in 1825 and "expressed his approbation of the exquisite workmanship of the whole" though he privately thought it inexcusable of Canova to have caught such a poor likeness. The less critical natives, however, fairly glowed with self-satisfaction at owning such a masterpiece.[3]

On the morning of June 21, 1831—a memorable day in the history of the state of North Carolina and a significant date in the history of American sculpture—the citizens of Raleigh were stirring early, breakfasting in the cool of the morning. Workmen were already tinkering with the silvery zinc plates on the new roof of the State House—an additional measure of fire prevention to protect the art treasures and documents of the state. But the preventive measures of the General Assembly went for nothing that day. A careless workman allowed some live coals to drop down through the roof into the attic, starting a fire that left the building a gutted ruin.

In the middle of that ruin lay the melancholy fragments of what had been the Canova Washington.[4] Though some of the state papers and some portraits had been saved, all efforts to move the statue proved unavailing. The fire leapt with such speed through the dry timbers of the building that the mortified and unfortunate populace could only stand silent around a pathetically useless little fire engine while the flames ate their way through the doomed fabric. For a moment the spectators could see the statue sitting impassive and majestic in a shower of falling brands and sparks, glowing with an almost supernatural light. Suddenly the roof sagged and caved, the flames roared higher and higher, shrouding the precious image in sheets of flame.

News of this deplorable disaster spread throughout the country. The details of the "awful conflagration" were announced in the New York papers on June 27th.[5] That same day Ball Hughes, an English sculptor newly arrived in New York, wrote to the Governor of North Carolina offering himself as one capable of restoring the burned fragments of the statue "so as to render the joins imperceptible." The loss of the statue was regarded as a national loss, and North Carolina was widely censured for her carelessness. Rumors of the high price the state had paid Canova were bandied about until in extreme exaggeration the statue was said to have cost $32,000, a truly colossal sum. Actually the price paid was something over $11,000, which was quite colossal enough considering that at the time the total annual expenditure of the state was only about $90,000.

Any number of people in Raleigh could remember that brave Fourth of July celebration back in 1815 when the idea of erecting a statue of Washington was first proposed. The American victories of the War of 1812 had fanned the fires of patriotism to a high pitch, and in a burst of enthusiasm the General Assembly had resolved that the state should purchase a statue of the Father of the Nation to adorn the State House.

Governor William Miller, somewhat overcome by the importance and complications of this unusual responsibility wrote to the state's senators in Washington for advice. The Assembly's resolution had given no indication of how much they were willing to spend or where to turn to find a sculptor, and sculptors were as rare as emperors in North Carolina at that time. The senators, puzzled by Governor Miller's request, addressed letters to all the eminent men they could think of who were noted for their refined sensibilities in matters of art and philosophy, asking advice upon this nice problem.

Was there a sculptor of sufficient ability and worthy of the honor then (1816) available in the United States? Where could one procure large blocks of white marble without flaw? How much should the state pay for its monument? Considered replies were gathered by the senators and forwarded to the Governor. Letters came from such men as Benjamin Latrobe, who was then en-

---

[3] See Frontispiece.
[4] These fragments are preserved today in the Hall of History, Raleigh, N. C.

[5] "The pride and glory of our city is no more! *The State House is reduced to ashes!*—its fine decorations—its Library—and, above all, the *chef d'œuvre* of Canova, the Statue of WASHINGTON are destroyed . . ." Quoted from the New York *American*, June 27, 1831. Extract from a letter to the editor of the *National Intelligencer* from Raleigh, N. C., June 21, 1831.

gaged upon the rebuilding of the national Capitol, and from William Jones, Secretary of the Navy, and from many others, all conveying suggestions. But the reply that carried the most weight came from Thomas Jefferson, who wrote:

Monticello, Jan. 22, [18]16

DEAR SIR

Your favor of the 7th after being a fortnight on the road, reached [me] this last night. On the subject of the statue of Genl. Washington which the legislature of N. Carolina has ordered to be procured, and set up in their capitol, I shall willingly give you my best information and opinions.

1. Your first inquiry is whether one worthy the character it is to represent, and the state which erects it, can be made in the United States? Certainly it cannot. I do not know that there is a single marble statuary[e] in the U. S. but I am sure there cannot be one who would offer himself as qualified to undertake this monument of gratitude and taste,—besides, no quarry of statuary marble has yet, I believe, been opened in the U. S., that is to say of a marble pure white, and in blocks of sufficient size, without flaw or vein. The quarry of Carara [*sic*] in Italy is the only one...

2. Who should make it? There can be but one answer to this. Old Canove of Rome. No artist in Europe would place himself in a line with him, and for 30 years, within my own knowledge, he has been considered by all Europe as without a rival. He draws his blocks from Carara, and delivers the statue compleat and packed for transportation at Rome...

3. Price, time, size, style? It will probably take a couple of years to be ready. I am not ... exact as to the price ... Yours should be something larger [than life-size]. The difference it makes in the impression can scarcely be conceived. As to the style or costume, I am sure the artist, and every person of taste in Europe would be for the Roman. ... Our boots and regimentals have a very puny effect. ... Canove's eminence will be a sensible ingredient in the price. I think that for such a statue ... you would have a good bargain from Canove at 7 or 8000 D. [dollars] and should not be surprized were he to require 10,000 D. ...

4. From what model? Ciracchi [*sic*] made a bust of General Washington in plaister. It was the finest which came from his hand, and my opinion of Ciracchi was that he was second to no living sculptor, except Canove. ... His style had been formed on the fine models of antiquity in Italy and he had caught their ineffable majesty of expression. ... After the death of Ciracchi, Mr. Appleton, our consul at Leghorn, a man of worth and taste, purchased of his widow the original plaister with a view to profit by copies of marble and plaister from it. He still has it at Leghorn, and it is the only original from which the statue can be formed. ...

5. Through whose agency? None so ready, or so competent as Mr. Appleton himself. He has had relations with Canove, is a judge of price, convenient to engage the work ... to receive and to forward it to N. Carolina. ... I particularize all these things, that you may not be surprised with after-claps of expense, not counted on before-hand. ... A letter from the Secretary of State to Mr. Appleton ... would not be without effect.

Accept the assurances of my great esteem and respect

TH:JEFFERSON

P. S. You mention that you shall communicate my letter to the Governor. To this I have no objection, provided it be kept out of the newspapers. But as I do not know to how many he may have to communicate it, I append this P. S. for your and his consideration only. Appleton has a friend and great favorite in a sculptor of the name of Bartholini, whom he thinks equal to Canove, and his friendship may lead him to find difficulties with Canove and draw the job to Bartholini, of whose name I have never heard but from Mr. Appleton. I could not yield to his opinion alone against that of all Europe. He should understand ... that it is particularly to the hand of Canove, and no other that they chuse to confide this work. ...

TH:J.[7]

Such a letter was apparently just what Governor Miller had hoped for. It provided for all possibilities—it not only recommended a sculptor but also suggested an agent already in Italy who was competent to deal with such a problem. Jefferson foresaw all difficulties, including the "after-claps of expense," and proposed a sound solution to the Governor's problem. But there is more to the letter than this—for in it we find quite simply outlined for us the prevailing notions about the plastic art which were current during the period of the formation of the first American school of sculpture. These ideas were to continue down the century to the time of the Civil War and they were to be the major influences in the lives and works of our sculptors. Italy was the land of sculpture; Canova, the Prince of Sculpture; the style was classic, the marble white, and the first patrons of the art were legislators— a notably powerful and articulate group.

In 1832, one year after the fire at Raleigh, Congress gave its first large commission to an *American* sculptor— they ordered a statue of Washington for the Rotunda of the Capitol from Horatio Greenough.

From that time forward political figures enter as an important factor in deciding and forwarding the careers

___

[e] That is, a sculptor.

[7] R. D. W. Conner, *Canova's Statue of Washington* (1910).

of almost every American sculptor. These happy artists, once their reputations were established, had powerful statesmen to push them forward. They reveled in incredibly lush commissions from cities, states, and nation. Sometimes the statesmen merely sat for their portraits, as Jackson did for Powers. Often they obtained government commissions for sculptors who were their friends. Thomas Crawford in this way received the largest commission given to any one artist of his time. Joel Hart made an entire career of turning out portrait busts and statues of Henry Clay. In New England the great domed brow of Daniel Webster was a favorite subject for sculptors. Stephen A. Douglas took a great interest in the career of Leonard Volk. John Rogers' groups were first widely publicized by Abolitionist orators. Charles Sumner and Edward Everett both played important parts in forwarding the careers of sculptors.

The statesmen, as patrons of sculptors, were very generous. Powers received $19,000 for his monument to Webster in Boston; Story was paid the astounding sum of $40,000 for a monument of Chief Justice Marshall. Almost every sculptor of the time had a design for a colossal monument to George Washington tucked away in some corner of his studio—just in case a monument committee might turn up. Thomas Ball found a wealthy private patron who purchased his design for a Washington Monument in order to present it to his native village in Massachusetts. Randolph Rogers received $50,000 for a Civil War monument in Rhode Island and $75,000 for a similar work for the state of Michigan. Henry Tuckerman records this fact with pleasure and says the states can charge this "to the account of public education"—and well they might. It was no wonder that more and more talented Yankee boys were attracted by the romantic and practical aspects of the art of sculpture.

Hiram Powers was quite wounded that Congress, when everyone else was singing his praises, never awarded him a commission. He thought that his European reputation should have made him automatically a sort of sculptor in chief to the United States. He poured out his ideas to one of his friends:

Will the government of the United States never learn, that there is no safeguard so effectual to our liberty and our Constitution, as the patriotism of our public men? And when will they learn that patriotism can never be so inflamed among the masses of the people, or its holy fires kept so bright on the altar of the Capitol, as by covering the consecrated soil of the nation, and surrounding the Capitol with the statues and monuments of illustrious men, who have devoted themselves to the glory of the country?[8]

If Powers' statue of Daniel Webster may be taken as his idea of what a public monument should be, we ought to be grateful that Congress did not give Hiram a chance to populate the city of Washington with his "old-clothes" statues. Jarves, the most acute critic of American art of the time, says:

If the ignorance of legislative bodies or the zeal of interested parties, at a heavy outlay of public funds, foists on the people works whose sole effect on the cultivated mind is disgust or ridicule, and on the common simply wonder at mechanical dexterity, bigness, or theatrical display, as in the instance of Clark Mills' equestrian statue at Washington, no protest is too strong; for such abortive work tends to bring all art into disrepute, even with the multitude. The desire for greatness is in itself a noble instinct, but in matters of art it must not be confused with bigness or mechanical skill.[9]

In 1843, Thomas Crawford wrote from Rome to his friends in New York: "I look to the formation of a pure school of Art in our glorious country. We have surpassed already the Republics of Greece in our political institutions, and I see no reason why we should not attempt to approach their excellence in the fine arts, which as much as anything, has secured undying fame to Grecian Genius."[10] The term "Grecian genius" rapidly became indispensible in discussing the lives and works of American sculptors.

The conservative and academic character of American sculpture in the early nineteenth century was, all things considered, unavoidable. First, perhaps, were the demands of the political patrons—since most of them were lawyers, it is only natural that in matters of art, as in matters of law, they should depend heavily on established precedents. Second, the artists themselves were timid, provincial amateurs of art; to them the faithful copy arrived at by a certain number of easily grasped mechanical shifts sufficed for the manufacture of statuary. Thus, it was articulate political bodies with public funds to spend on national symbols that helped to create the demand for sculpture in America, and gave to the art a

[8] C. E. Lester, *The Artist* (1845). [Not an actual quotation by Powers but most certainly inspired by him.]
[9] J. J. Jarves, *Art Idea* (1864).
[10] Thomas Hicks, *Eulogy on Thomas Crawford* (1865).

special honorable national significance. By passing resolutions and appropriating rewarding sums for sculpture, a whole era in American taste was ordained. The pursuit of "high art" in the form of sculpture, formerly an exotic mystery with Royalist and idolatrous overtones, suddenly became a patriotic, legal, remunerative occupation. American ingenuity, unwilling to be outdone by Europe in anything, arose to the task.

2 · PORTRAIT BUST
or, Sculptors and Art Patrons

Story's work as a sculptor speaks, incontestably, of the public it had to confront and involves a view of that public. There are things in the arts . . . that have more eloquence and value for us by that reference than they offer in any other way . . .

HENRY JAMES, *William Wetmore Story and His Friends*

Now that the stories of sculptural subject matter are dimmed by time and the artists themselves are hazy figures as best, their sculpture, as Henry James suggests, speaks to us most clearly on the subject of the patrons of the art. It is a stony commentary on the people who paid hard cash for white marble and on the connoisseurs and art lovers who praised and enjoyed it. The artist, whether he likes it or not, is always the victim and beneficiary of the desires of his patrons. It is almost impossible for an artist to exist without patronage, and very rarely has he the power—or misfortune, as the case may be—to create in a mode beyond the tastes of his patron, because patron and artist alike are of the essence of their own time.

Most of the American patrons of art in the early nineteenth century were, in political matters, rabidly American, but in cultural matters the social patterns of the English gentry were closely followed. When the colonies became states, the men of wealth and education continued to look to Europe for guidance in taste just as their wives looked to Paris for the latest fashions in dress.

On the American cultural frontier in the early nineteenth century, sculpture had certain well-defined associations which governed the demands of the patrons of the art. These demands were conditioned not only by European precedents, but also by the patrons' experience and familiarity with the sculpture—such as it was—that was to be found upon the American scene.

Perhaps the most powerful and widespread association with sculpture in the American mind was that of tombstones, cemeteries, and death. The early sculptors gravitated naturally to the marble yards and quarries where tombstones were cut. To a generation believing that life was but a prelude to the grave, an almost Egyptian preparation for the hereafter, the selection, design, and placing of one's tombstone was a major event. In the picturesque rural cemeteries, which had by 1840 become an important adjunct to every self-respecting town, marble angels mourned, marble willows wept, marble doves descended, and obelisks pointed their monitory fingers to heaven. Intensely mournful sentiments supported the themes of the sorrowful stones. Only on the headstone of the town wit, perhaps an old disciple of Tom Paine, could be found inscribed such a bit of frontier flippancy as "Grind on Ye Devils."

The rural cemetery was the idea of Jacob Bigelow, a Boston physician and botanist, who became alarmed at the overcrowded condition of the city's small churchyard burying grounds, which he believed menaced the health of the entire community. In 1831, with the help of the Massachusetts Horticultural Society he organized the Mount Auburn Cemetery Company. The Company purchased a plot of land known as Sweet Auburn, on the outskirts of Cambridge, a wooded eminence overlooking the tidal flats of the Charles River. There they proceeded to lay out a combined graveyard and botanical garden. It was an excellent idea and in no time every American city had at least one rural cemetery modeled on the Mount Auburn plan.

As the century took its toll of men of the Revolutionary generation, the cemeteries gradually became filled with elegant memorials. Mount Auburn became a sort of Valhalla-on-the-Charles as its ivied chapel added, one by one, the memorial effigies of famous men. Slowly the family plots were ornamented until the ever-gathering marmoreal company transformed a simple graveyard into a Yankee Campo Santo, an out-of-door sculpture museum and botanical park given special meaning by the presence of the vast and distinguished company underground. These rural cemeteries were indeed influential, later in the century, in formulating the conception of public parks—which are, in a sense, cemeteries embellished with sculpture, but minus the corpses.

It is hard for us to imagine a tour of Greenwood Cemetery as an attraction of the first interest to the tourist visiting New York, but in the last century (even up to the eighties and nineties) it was so considered. In Boston, of course, one went to see Mount Auburn, and in Philadelphia there was Laurel Hill. These were numbered among the most interesting and beautiful attractions of their respective towns. The city guidebooks of the time often devote more space to descriptions of local cemeteries than they do to any other single feature of the metropolis.

Poets wrote many a line praising the sylvan beauties of these hallowed places . . .

Here may the heart, half desolate and broken,
  Far from the city's pomp its vigil keep,
And wreathe with the fairest flowers, affections token,
  The pale cold marble, where its loved ones sleep.

Special guidebooks were compiled which pointed out the grassy glades and rustic dells, or eminences from which a picturesque view of the whole "white city" might be obtained. The more noteworthy monuments were described . . .

. . . To the admirers of architecture, this monument will prove a treat . . . Proceeding eastward, we view the classic tomb erected over the remains of Claribelle Lyndon, daughter of Jonas and Hannah Lyndon. This exquisite work of art is from the chisel of Joseph Maples, Esq., sculptor, and is a most beautiful specimen of American Art. It is undoubtedly the gem of North Laurel Hill. . . . Innumerable monuments are tastefully disposed in this neighborhood—some of them being exquisite works of art . . . Among the tombs is the figure of a lovely child, a masterpiece of the celebrated sculptor Pettrich. It is much visited and admired. No less beautiful, though more humble in pretension, is that to "OUR DEAR WILLIE" . . . We must now bid adieu to this delightful place—

Where perchance, our footsteps never
  Its fairy haunts again in life may tread;
Yet, as a gem, in memory's casket ever
  Art thou enshrined, oh, loveliest city of the dead.[1]

The fine points of Greenwood versus Laurel Hill or Mount Auburn were actively argued and compared. Tickets of admission were distributed among the friends of owners of family plots. On clear days the gate keeper's lodge at the cemetery was surrounded with carriages which had brought elegant ladies and gentlemen to stroll in the parklike enclosure and admire the natural and artificial beauties of the "garden of graves." If many of our sculptors learned their craft in the marble yards of Guion (Cincinnati), Launitz (New York), or Sisson

(Baltimore), it may be taken for granted that almost all of the patrons of sculptors drew a large part of whatever understanding and familiarity they had with the art of sculpture from the dismal exhibits in the cemetery. If our early sculptors spent their lives creating "a death which they called poetic," as Emerson says, perhaps it was because the physical death of the graveyard was so intimately associated with sculpture in the minds of both patron and artist . . . it is small wonder then that little was produced before 1860 that was, sculpturally, above the commercial tombstone level.

To the cool critical eye of James Jackson Jarves the famous rural cemeteries had quite a different aspect from that usually recorded. He writes in 1864:

Mount Auburn, lovely and spiritual in some respects, speaks too loudly of property, exclusion, and building, things of the earth, instead of the symbolism of heaven. The artistic tone of the cemetery is mechanical, heavy, and cold. There is little or no original invention or evidence of right feeling in its monuments, very little that proclaims Christian faith. A philosopher of no creed might wander long about it unable to decide whether the pagan, pantheistic spirit, the mere mercantile, practical, or skeptical modern feeling, the sectarian sentiment, or the family desire to honor the dead, predominated. He would see a great display of names, not unfrequently conjoined after the manner of mercantile firms, and an immense expenditure in iron and stone guiltless of aesthetic taste . . . much bastard pagan and classical design. . . . As yet, however, whenever [cemeteries] are pretentious and expensive, like Mount Auburn and Greenwood, they fail in spiritual essentials and proprieties.[2]

Yet the cemetery was not the only place where the drama of death associated itself with the art of sculpture on the frontier. There existed still another school for artist and patron alike—a place where all the obvious elements that led to the making of images and all the elements that the public regarded as virtues in sculpture were fused. This was in the Waxworks Museum, which, for so many years—even down to the present century—formed such an entertaining feature of life in the metropolis. Here were displayed, with repellantly fascinating reality, the scenes of "moral dramas," the effigies of national heroes, bloody battle scenes, and the grim visages of the latest murderers to be hanged in the locality. Here too were portraits of fashionable actors and actresses, gesturing in the dramatic crises of their favorite roles.

---

[1] *Strangers Guide in Philadelphia* (1860).

[2] Jarves, *The Art Idea* (1864).

The morbidities of the waxworks chamber of horrors were easily transferred in the waxy marbles of the neo-classic school of sculpture to the parlors of "the big house on the hill." To the wives of successful merchants and manufacturers a piece of white marble statuary was a symbol of refinement and culture. No drawing room was complete without an "ideal figure" or bust to add tone to the embellishments of the room. An admirer of Hiram Powers writes: ". . . I would recommend a copy of the *Proserpine,* which I promise *any lady* shall be more perfect than herself. For a *boudoir* there is nothing so beautiful, and a more classic conception could not adorn a library. It is an exquisite ideal female bust, resting in a basket of Acanthus leaves, and it forms, perhaps, the gem of his studio . . ." (1845).[3]

It had been hard for young Americans to find sculpture to study at home in the early days except in the graveyards and waxworks. Clevenger, in order to get plaster casts to copy, crept into a Cincinnati cemetery by night to steal impressions from a monument made by an itinerant master. Small collections of casts from the antique were to be found of course—carefully veiled, and shown separately on alternate days to ladies and gentlemen. But they were hard to see, as most of them were kept in such exclusive retreats as the Pennsylvania Academy of Fine Arts in Philadelphia. There were casts, too, in the Boston Athenaeum and a few in the stuffy little institutions of New York. But one could hardly say that students were encouraged by the proprietors of these institutions to study their casts. By 1860, however, the active patronage of American sculptors working in Florence and Rome had somewhat amended this situation. Many travelers who made the grand tour brought home marbles and casts which they lent for annual exhibitions in the local Academy, Athenaeum, or Mechanics Institute.

The exhibition and gallery catalogues of the day not only described each item at length . . . "carved from a single block of purest Carrara" . . . but they threw in a complete scenario or brief novella in three paragraphs telling the story, setting the emotional tone, to assist the art lover to approach each piece of statuary in the right frame of mind. These marbles might easily be thought of as "snapshots" of scenes in a play. Emerson derides the sculpture of his contemporaries thus: "The art of sculp-

ture has long ago perished to any real effect . . . in the works of our plastic arts, and especially of sculpture, creation is driven into a corner. I cannot hide from myself that there is a certain paltriness, as of toys, and the trumpery of the theatre in sculpture."[4]

Perhaps it is only natural that so much of the sculpture of his time should be found today in the ornate lobbies and lounges of that sublimated waxworks—the modern movie palace. If the waxworks was a dead theater, sculpture of the American neo-classic school was little more than a glorified waxworks, refined and englamored by the pure Carrara marble and romanticized by being made by an exiled genius in the studio workshops of Florence and Rome so far away across the sea.

Each generation discovers for itself that sculpture is dead. Emerson discovered it in the forties, Hawthorne discovered it in the fifties, Jarves discovered it in the sixties. It really seems rather unkind of the literary men to announce their discovery in public with such persistency when the sculptors have labored so faithfully to translate and illustrate literature in marble and bronze. Perhaps to the authors it seemed unnecessarily primitive to revert again to writing on stone when paper had been proven only little less permanent.

Literary sculpture is certainly the most cumbersome form of record known to man, and in attempting it the sculptor lays himself open to a double death at the hands of later generations, who, in their modernity, dismiss both the style of his school of sculpture and his taste in literature with condescension and sneers. Though the sculptors of the Classico-Jacksonian school molded their clay on the finest themes of antiquity and found inspiration in the best literature of their day, one can scarcely decipher the stories they wanted to tell. While New England authors were flourishing, the sculptors were producing a sentimental literature in marble. Van Wyck Brooks says, "The drapery of Cleopatra as Story conceived her, was almost a novel in itself."[5] Today the point of obscure biblical legends and classical myths is almost totally lost on a generation of non-churchgoers that also pays scant attention to classical learning. In 1850 the tragedy of Rizpah (a biblical heroine) was familiar to everyone, and genteel conversation and literature were thickly sprinkled with allusions to the ancient Greek and

[3] C. E. Lester, *The Artist* . . . (1845).

[4] Emerson, *Essays.* 1st series, Art.
[5] *The Flowering of New England* (1938).

Roman gods of "idolatrous times." In 1855 Thomas Bulfinch, the son of the Boston architect, published his famous mythology and the gods and heroes of antiquity became familiar to every schoolboy. The book was an invaluable source of inspiration to sculptors looking for "new" subject matter.

Though several large political commissions were awarded to sculptors during the period they were, of course, not quite everyday occurrences. Most of the sculptors sustained themselves between times by the manufacture of portrait busts. "A lucrative business" Hiram Powers called it. His profits enabled him to build a home and studio in Florence, where he supported a family of seven or eight children in the finest style. One Yankee sculptor is reputed to have made no less than three hundred portrait busts.

An English traveler who toured the States in the late thirties remarked that American interest in art seemed to him to be confined exclusively to portraiture. A poetess of the time gives us a clue to this passion for marble immortality that caused so many busts to be made:

The dread power of heaven alone can restore
    That life to the dead, which it gave them before;
But man's lofty genius can rescue from death,
    The last lovely look, the last smile, the last breath.
The sculptor, in marble, a life can restore,
    That never will perish til time be no more;
Thus the great, the ingenious, the lovely and pure,
    For example, applause, and affection endure.[6]

There was a special exclusiveness in being "done" in white marble that had a peculiar appeal to men of wealth. Sculptors traveled about the country "taking likenesses" by the dozen; there was money in it. It was just like being photographed—and almost as mechanical. During a two-year residence in Albany, New York, Henry Kirke Brown executed forty portrait busts. When Hiram Powers sailed for Italy he took with him no less than thirteen portraits in clay to be "put into marble." "The love of busts," we are told, "was generally diffused."

Hawthorne notes the American passion for marble busts in his description of a sculptor's studio in *The Marble Faun*:

There were also several portrait busts, comprising those of two or three of the illustrious men of our own country, whom Kenyon, before he left America, had asked permission to model. He had done so, because he sincerely believed that,

[6] Cornelia A. Walter, in *Rural Cemeteries of America* (1847).

whether he wrought the busts in marble or bronze, the one would corrode and the other crumble, in the long lapse of time, beneath these great men's immortality. Possibly, however, the young artist may have under-estimated the durability of his material. Other faces there were, too, of men who (if the brevity of remembrance, after death, can be argued from their little value in life) should have been represented in snow rather than marble. Posterity will be puzzled what to do with busts like these, the concretions and petrifactions of a vain self-estimate; but will find, no doubt, that they serve to build into stone walls, or burn into quicklime, as well as if the marble had never been blocked into the guise of human heads.

But it is an awful thing, indeed, this endless endurance, this almost indestructability, of a marble bust! Whether in our own case, or that of other men, it bids us sadly measure the little, little time, during which our lineaments are likely to be of interest to any human being. It is especially singular that Americans should care about perpetuating themselves in this mode. The brief duration of our families, as a hereditary household, renders it next to a certainty that the great-grand-children will not know their father's grandfather, and that half a century hence, at farthest, the hammer of the auctioneer will thump its knock-down blow against his blockhead, sold at so much for the pound of stone! And it ought to make us shiver, the idea of leaving our features to be a dusty white ghost among strangers of another generation who will take our nose between their thumb and fingers (as we have seen men do by the Caesar's) and infallibly break it off, if they can do so without detection!

The sculptors often complained that commissions for portrait busts left them no time for "ideal" works. Oftentimes a popular man would be swamped with orders for busts two or three years in advance. But somehow they found time for works of the imagination, usually by raising their prices.

In those days many a young sculptor made his precarious way toward fame by turning out miniature portrait busts—"cabinet busts," they were called—at twenty-five dollars a head. In the eighteen forties and fifties it was the fashion to have copies of these made in sufficient quantity to distribute as mementos among one's friends. This charming custom, however, came rapidly to an end when the less expensive daguerreotype ousted the marble keepsake from its place of honor among the seashells on the whatnot.

Naturally among the patrons of art and the public generally the prudes had a great deal to say about sculpture—the common attitude is described to us by Jarves:

There was an intermediate state of unintelligent curiosity

about art as something strange or wonderful, like a newly discovered plant or a gorilla from Africa. This was the time when people curious to know what the *Chanting Cherubs* of Greenough or the *Greek Slave* of Powers could be, were scarcely to be persuaded to visit them lest their modesty be shocked at their nudity, or were led to go because they were naked, and peep at them between their fingers. . . .[7]

The *Chanting Cherubs*, commissioned by James Fenimore Cooper, when they were shown at the Boston Athenaeum in 1831, caused a flurry of horror among the pure minded—these innocuous infants were naked! Greenough pointed out at the time that the same American public that was shocked by this display willingly paid enormous sums to gaze without alarm at the "lascivious" fandango dancers (Fanny Elssler *et al.*) imported from Vienna or Paris—he considered it "a measure of our appetite for the meretricious."[8]

After Charles Sumner had visited Greenough's studio to see the progress on his statue of Washington he wrote to the sculptor warning him what to expect from the American public when they found that Greenough had represented Washington partly clothed like a Roman god. Sumner says:

Let me congratulate you on the completion of your statue. . . . It will give you fame. Still, I feel that it must pass through a disagreeable ordeal,—one which, as it seems unavoidable, I hope will not be annoying to you. I refer to the criticisms of people knowing nothing about art. In Europe, an artist is judged at once, in a certain sense, by his peers. With us, we are all critics. The people will not hesitate to judge your work; and some will perhaps complain, that Washington is naked. . . . The loungers in the Rotunda . . . many before never having seen a statue in marble,—will want the necessary knowledge to enable them to appreciate your "Washington." Should you not prepare them, so far as you can? And you can do a great deal. Publish . . . some of the papers you read to me during my visit to Florence,—particularly that on the "Nude"; for there, I think, you will encounter a deal of squeamish criticism.[9]

In 1847, when Hiram Powers' *Greek Slave* was shown in New York, his canny business agent came forearmed against the prudes with published eulogiums on the *Slave* by English art critics and, better still, with a voluminous

pamphlet quoting at length the approving remarks of the Reverend Mr. Dewey. This gentleman of the cloth claimed that the statue (though obviously quite naked) was "clothed all over with sentiment, sheltered, protected by it, from every profane eye. Brocade, cloth of gold, could not be a more complete protection than the vesture of holiness in which she stands." When the *Slave* was shipped to Cincinnati for exhibition in 1847 she was met by a body of local clergymen who "gave her a 'character'" and recommended, after due examination of the problem, that she could be exhibited without bringing "the blush of shame" to "the cheek of modesty." But even with all this approval from the guardians of public morals some horrid Boston artist had the effrontery to say that the *Slave* was plainly lascivious and that artistically it had nothing else to recommend it. It is heartening to note, however, that the American public of the time had no monopoly on prudery; in 1853 a cast of the Venus de Milo was tried in a court of law in Mannheim, Germany, on the charge of nudity, and she was convicted there and condemned.

On comparing the cost of making sculpture and the prices the patrons paid for it, one of the principal attractions which turned so many men to sculpture as a means of making a living becomes clear. In the matter of payment the patrons were most generous and pleasantly uncritical.

Jarves says: "So far as the stimulus of buying is concerned the American sculptor is the most fortunate of modern artists. If ample patronage can create a national school, we shall have one soon. But the demand having preceded knowledge and skill, we are obtaining our sculpture to the detriment of our taste. It forces an inept art on an unprepared public."[10]

Jarves further reports the economics of sculpture thus: "The cost of making an ideal bust in Florence, including the marble, like the usual run of fancy heads, is eighty to one hundred dollars, by contract. A portrait bust, life size costs higher, and is less remunerative because seldom repeated, but two hundred dollars would cover the cost of the bust . . . repetitions of the ordinary parlor statues, Eves, Greek Slaves, Judiths, and their like, from $800 to $1,000. The profit on large monuments is so large as to turn towards sculpture considerable busi-

[7] Jarves, *Art Thoughts* (1875).
[8] Tuckerman, *The Book of the Artists* (1869).
[9] Pierce, *Memoir and Letters of Charles Sumner* (1878). (The letter is dated February 1841.)

[10] *Art Thoughts* (1869).

ness talent, which, as regards art, had better be left to its common pursuits."[11]

Powers at the height of his fame received $1,000 apiece for his portrait busts. He is reputed to have made altogether about 150 of these. He sold *fifty copies* of his "ideal" bust of *Proserpine* at $400 each. For his *Greek Slave* (of which six replicas were made) he received about $4,000 each. In 1858 Mr. Astor paid $7,500 for his *California*. Powers received $19,000 for his Webster monument in Boston, on which his profit is estimated at $16,000, certainly a very tidy sum for one of the most commonplace effigies ever constructed.

Estimating merely from the figures that have been published, Hiram Powers must have made well over $200,000 during the thirty-six years he lived in Florence —an average yearly income of well over $5,000. This was a truly handsome figure when one considers the very low cost of living in Italy in the mid-nineteenth century.

When a copy of the *Greek Slave* was sold at auction in New York in 1858 for $6,000, Powers wrote to the auctioneer, who had informed him of the sale, "The price you obtained for the statue is much greater than the sum originally paid for it, and when an artist's work succeeds so well at public auction, he cannot but feel encouraged, and thankful too, for public opinion so *substantially* expressed."[12]

Something seemed to happen to the American businessmen of 1850 when they went on a tour of Europe in search of health and rest after the exhaustion of business life in America. They seemed to become suddenly victims of "the art infection" and they bought pictures and commissioned statues in Italy that they never would have considered as much of an investment at home. A whole tribe of hotelkeepers and broken-down noblemen sold them "old masters" by the yard, and they paid round sums for elegant copies of the most famous masterpieces—Raphael's *Madonna of the Chair* was often "engaged" for weeks in advanced by artists who spent their lives copying in the galleries. But for sculpture American businessmen turned to the Yankee exiles. It was remarked that "the taste for sculpture seems to be growing of late, and especially among the Americans. They buy more statues, I am told, than any other na-

tion."[13] Apparently they bought so much sculpture that the painters became alarmed—at least one of them wrote in a peevish vein:

It seems to me that sculpture has risen above par, of late [1847]: painters are but an inferior grade of artists. This exaltation of sculpture above painting, which in this country has prevailed, is unjust, and has never been acknowledged in the past. There is no necessity of insisting upon the superior claims of either, and particularly those of sculpture, for they are least tenable.

Taking painting in all its departments, its influence is certainly more extensive than that of sculpture: and to excell in painting requires a combination of a greater number of faculties than to excell in sculpture. Sculpture is more limited. He who cannot distinguish one color from another may be a sculptor. I only intend to say that undue importance has been given lately to sculpture. . . .

Yours truly, but in haste,

Thomas Cole[14]

Of the businessmen patrons Mr. Jarves again has something pertinent to say:

As most patrons are business men, who buy on the whim of the moment, without having bestowed any serious consideration on art, they are readily attracted by those mental qualities and personal habits most in accord with their own. Mistaking secondary for primary effects, they are easily put into sympathy with the business artist, who is so intelligible in his speech and acts and whose works have a prosaic character or material aim. . . .[15]

Doubtless the businessmen who went to Hiram Powers' studio in Florence understood very well his system of bill collecting. When a patron was slow in paying for his portrait bust, it was ignominiously displayed on a shelf at the entrance of the studio and labeled "Delinquent" for all the stream of noted visitors to see. Hiram called this shelf his "pillory."

The art unions and art associations so popular in the middle of the century distributed busts and statuettes broadcast over the country to the lucky winners in their annual lotteries. In 1855 when the *Greek Slave* was offered as the grand prize by the Cosmopolitan Art Association in New York, the possibility of becoming the proud possessor of the fair Greek brought flocks of new subscribers into the Association. A Mrs. Kate Gillespie

[11] *Ibid.*
[12] *Cosmopolitan Art Journal,* II (Dec. 1857).
[13] W. W. Story, *Conversation in a Studio* (1890).
[14] L. L. Noble, *The Course of Empire* (1853).
[15] *Art Thoughts.*

of Brady's Bend, Pennsylvania, was the fortunate winner that year, and for a while Hiram Powers' masterpiece was the most awesome thing in Lycoming County. After she had had her fill of the *Greek Slave,* and had made a tidy sum by exhibiting it, Mrs. Gillespie sent the statue back to New York, where it was exhibited at the Merchants Exchange and there sold at auction for $6,000 before a large crowd of bidders.

In 1858 the Cosmopolitan Art Association distributed as premiums over one hundred pieces of "modern" sculpture. These prizes went to all part of the country: *Psyche* to San Francisco, *The Nymph of the Arno* to Chicago, *Fidelity* to New Orleans. "It is thus the Asso-CIATION speeds its Art-ministers over the country, upon their perpetual mission of good. We trust the fortunate possessors of these charming marbles will hold them accessible to the public of their respective places."[16]

Sculpture was distributed through the country by yet another means in the eighteen fifties and sixties. Enterprising Italian plaster workers in New York and Chicago caught on to the American hankering for sculpture and began to turn out thousands of little busts and figurines of Daniel Webster, Jenny Lind, Napoleon, and currently notorious murderers. These they peddled from door to door in large baskets or on trays balanced on the head. When John Rogers first started in the statuary business in New York, he too adopted this method of selling. Artemus Ward accused the Italian "busters" of making the same bust over and over again, merely changing the name to suit the occasion. Sometimes it was Webster, sometimes it was "Cole the Wife-Pizener," but, he claimed, it was always the same bust.

The patrons of sculptors knew what they wanted— and, as is the way of patrons, they wanted what they knew. Apparently they loved white marble for itself alone regardless of subject or skill or sculpture. To us it may seem as though they got what they deserved, but perhaps we should not be too hasty in passing judgments in matters of taste. Whatever it was they wanted and got —we are the happy heirs.

The sculptor, who perhaps suffered in this respect more than any other artist, was the innocent or willing dupe of the demands of his patrons. Their interpretation of tradition naturally became his. Their standards were forced upon him by economic necessity if not by his lack of training. In the tumultuous riot of frontier society financial success was almost the only fixed index of a man's place in the social structure. To most of the patrons of sculptors financial success in art seemed a sure indication of immortal genius. They envisioned a marble group, "Mechanical and Commercial Virtue" in the guise of two classic gods, a treasure to stand in the parlor. Supported there in that Victorian sanctum, posed securely on the weighty pedestal of success, the deities displayed conspicuously their emblems and attributes, recognized by all—a bolt of ligtning, for speedy execution; a mirror, for vanity and fidelity to externals; the endless belt, for mass production; calipers, scales, and rule, for accuracy and dextrous balancing tricks; a broken column, symbol of ancient Greece for modern gods to lean upon. The whole a sterile and patented formula, a monument to the perversion of native ingenuity and adaptability.

In a sense the melancholy machines turned out by the sculptors of the nineteenth century are somewhat akin to the "art-machines" of the present day abstract sculptors. If the works of Hiram Powers cause us to smile from our cultural pinnacle, what will future generations do when confronted with some of the sculpture of today? What indeed? These new parlor machines do not even distill the syrup of sentiment—can one be sure of finding any significance whatever in a "construction" of sheet metal and string? What fascinating conclusions are not open to the critic a hundred years from now?

WARNING

TO CONNOISSEURS AND ART PATRONS

☛ A vast amount of foreign marble is finding market in this country—chiefly the work of students in the studios of Florence, Roma, Genoa, & c. It is not, as a general thing, particularly good nor particularly bad, though it does sometimes victimize a *green* purchaser. Parties should be chary of purchasing until they are sure of what they buy.

Cosmopolitan Art Journal, March, 1860.

---

[16] *Cosmopolitan Art Journal,* II (March–June 1858).

3 · STATUARY GROUP
or, Whittler's Progress

In the names—POWERS, GREENOUGH, CRAWFORD—we should take pride, for it is they who lead the van of the band of Art-workers who are to give to America that love for marbles which shall render her, ere long, the repository for much that is great and worthy. What strides have we not already made in the development of our taste for the Fine Arts! and, counting on a future of constant progression, what may we not promise ourselves in the way of Art patronage and Art Culture!

Cosmopolitan Art Journal, 1857

WHEN one considers the background of our group of sculptors, their appearance on the American scene in such a brief space of time seems more and more amazing as a frontier phenomenon. The majority of them were the sons of farmers—Powers, Ives, Clevenger, Brown, Brackett, MacDonald, Rinehart, and Simmons. Others were the sons of small tradesmen and mechanics. Thomas Ball was the son of an impecunious sign painter, Rimmer, the son of a cobbler. Only Horatio and Richard Greenough and William Story were the sons of men of wealth and education—all the rest came from humble homes, hauling themselves up by their own bootstraps, some reaching the very pinnacle of international fame and fortune. In the eighteen thirties a sculptor's career seemed suddenly to offer sufficient inducement in cash, honor, and romance to attract these young men to make it their life work.

Considering the obstacles first placed in the way of the aspiring young sculptor in America more than a hundred years ago, it is indeed remarkable that anyone took up the art, and that by 1840 one could hear the phrase "the American School of Sculpture" or, better still, somewhat later, "the peculiar American genius for expression in marble." When John Trumbull was running his own little private "Royal Academy" in New York about 1820, he saw fit to encourage a hopeful young stonecutter,[1] who had come to him for advice, with the remark that "nothing in sculpture would be wanted in this country for yet a hundred years"[2]—a remark Trumbull lived to see refuted again and again. He was quite wrong, Americans wanted sculpture, or at least something that passed for

[1] Frazee.
[2] William Dunlap, *History of the Rise and Progress of the Arts of Design in the United States* (1834).

sculpture. They even carried it with them to the wildest frontiers and counted the labor of transportation as nothing.

If we "look on sculpture as history" with Mr. Emerson, we find reflected in polished marble, a valuable and oftentimes entertaining record of the ideals and enthusiasms of a period in American history which we are just beginning to appreciate. As social and human documents the sculptors' lives and works take on a new importance. They illuminate the sad history of the triumph of the machine over the artist and craftsman who struggles to find a place in the essentially hostile environment of an expanding frontier. There the unfettered freedoms of life in a cultural and geographical wilderness evolved, in perplexing contradiction, an exaggerated bondage to convention simultaneously with an unhappy liberation from long sustained tradition.

These early men had none of the advantages that most modern artists enjoy. Although there were a few art academies in the larger cities in 1830, they were rather half-heartedly run and were principally for the benefit of the painters. The only school to which the young sculptors could turn for encouragement, training, and companionship were the marble yards of tombstone cutters.

Some men seem to have picked up the rudiments of the sculptor's art wherever they happened to be. Very few of them had the advantage of early training at an academy of art. Some of them developed into sculptors by being apprenticed to woodcarvers and stonecutters after demonstrating some talent in that line (or a lack of talent at farming). Those with stronger mechanical inclinations approached sculpture from the waxworks, clock factory, machine shop, or carpenter's bench. Some were merely adept at the time-honored Yankee art of whittling. The majority of our sculptors who came from farms or small rural settlements never saw a piece of sculpture until they were grown men.

There must have been something classic in the sweet airs of Cincinnati in the decade 1830–1840 that made it such a favored nursery of the arts for at least a half dozen of our sculptors. As one traveler put it "sculpture seems peculiarily cherished in Cincinnati." The little Queen City of the West, bustling with river traffic and an expanding trade in real estate and hogs, already boasted two museums even as early as 1828, and a few years later a ladies' art association was going full blast, holding annual exhibitions and adding an elevating tone to the cultural life of the western metropolis. The town directories always listed private homes where works of art could be seen by such connoisseurs as found themselves upon the frontier. From Cincinnati came the sculptors Powers, Brackett, Clevenger, Brown, Frankenstein, Jones, and King. None of them was born there but they all first tried their hands at modeling there and for a brief moment they formed what might be called "the Cincinnati School." Powers was the chief inventor of waxworks and automata in the Western Museum, an adept at "that barbarous branch of art," the making of wax effigies. Clevenger received most of his training in the stoneyards of David Guion, the leading tombstone carver in the vicinity. Most of these men came under the influence of an obscure German craftsman[3] who introduced them to the mysteries of modeling and casting in plaster.

Most of our early sculptors never enjoyed more than a fragmentary common-school education—Clevenger seems to have escaped the birch rod and the three R's almost entirely, and his education was said to consist in a careful perusal of the *Penny Magazine of Useful Knowledge* and a keen attention to the conversation of the famous men who sat to him. His charm of manner and enthusiasm for the art carried him over all the rough spots, winning him a new friend and admirer every time he made a portrait bust. Erastus Dow Palmer made up for his lack of education by having his wife read to him from the works of Cooper, Irving, Scott, and Dickens while he was at work cutting cameos.

At the opposite end of the educational scale stands William Wetmore Story, Harvard A. B. '38, L. L. B. '40. Later in his life he was given honorary degrees by the venerable universities of Oxford and Bologna. Thomas Ball, though almost as unschooled as his fellows, rejoiced in an honorary degree from Dartmouth, awarded to him for his popular busts of distinguished alumni—Daniel Webster and Rufus Choate—not to mention President Lord.

Though we consider these men as sculptors, their talents and interests range over a wide field of endeavor. They were adept in the best Yankee style at many things besides their chosen field. As most of the sculpture of the day was heavily literary it is not surprising to find that a number of our sculptors appear as authors; at least two of them produced literary works that still retain a certain amount of interest beyond that of mere curiosities.[4] Almost all of them at one time or another composed poems, jingles, odes, and, of course, epitaphs. Many of them did passable drawings and paintings, and some started on their careers in art as miniature painters and silhouette cutters. Some were carpenters, engineers, architects, or just plain mechanics. One, as a surveyor, helped lay out the expanding western railroads; one wrote learnedly of the law. One became so interested in the conservation of wild life he gave up sculpture altogether to become chairman of the government Commission on Land Fisheries, in which capacity he served for twenty-seven years. Two were successful businessmen who deserted the marts of trade for the business of "high art," which they proceeded to turn into a financially successful enterprise.

Almost every one invented something (other than "sculptured Thoughts"); a patent file for working plaster, a machine for punching holes in metal, a measuring device, a new modeling mixture, a pointing machine to speed up the processes of the studio, an improved gun lock, a counting device, a fish-hatching trap, an unbreakable trunk that even the most powerful baggageman could not smash. They were always tinkering with something mechanical, some invention or ingenious contrivance that "would pay well if exploited," and they all depended heavily on mechanical means for making and reproducing sculpture.

One of the sculptors supported himself in the early stages of his career, when commissions were too far apart for comfort, by singing bass in the choirs around Boston, where he also developed a certain local fame as a participant in the oratorio concerts that were such an important feature of the cultural life in Boston in the fifties and sixties. Though none of the other sculptors were professional musicians, many of them had a polite interest in that art—at least enough to take part in parlor musicales.

---

[3] Eckstein.

[4] Horatio Greenough and W. W. Story.

Many of them showed marked talent for amateur theatricals and mimicry, not to mention showmanship, qualities that played an important part in the staging of their dramas in stone. William Wetmore Story, perhaps the most talented of the amateur thespians, also wrote dramas and with his friends performed them in his private theater in the Palazzo Barberini. He was also the most prolific author in the group, and the one who, perhaps, had least to say as a sculptor. In the seventies and eighties his poetical works, echoing the Brownings and Tennyson, were all the rage.

There seems to be in the personality of every sculptor a latent or partially developed interest in medicine. This was of course naturally stimulated by the study of anatomy which is a necessity of the sculptor's craft. The manner and degree of the development of this interest throws a revealing side light upon the character of the men and their work. In our group Theodatus Garlick, Horatio Stone, and William Rimmer all became practicing physicians. Garlick, more of a doctor than the other two, carried his interest in sculpture to its ultimate medical conclusion in plastic surgery. Horatio Stone divided his career at the age of forty, abandoning his medical practice in New York for the sculptor's life in the art world at Washington in 1848. William Rimmer, the best artist of the three doctors, was noted for his skill in treating typhoid cases. His knowledge of human anatomy was so sound it enabled him, as an artist, to create and compose using the human form with absolute freedom, a skill which none of the other sculptors could even approach. On the other hand, Hiram Powers was a natural-born "bone-doctor" with an implicit trust in nostrums and cure-alls, his knowledge of anatomy was superficial as that of a medicine man. Story's study of anatomy enabled him to write a book upon the subject—unfortunately for him as a sculptor, he was in all things essentially a literary man—in which he propounded some extraordinary theories on proportion based on researches into classical literature rather than on sound practice. Brackett's interest in anatomy and the study of nature led him into the field of biology, where he experimented in breeding game birds and fish with which to stock the forests and streams of his native New England. Clevenger's interest in anatomy was apparently passed on to his son, who became a noted doctor.

Some of the sculptors in the group were not only artists but also patrons of art in one way or another. At least four of them, following the precedent of Canova, left the contents of their studios, and funds, for the foundation or profit of art institutions back home. Randolph Rogers left the collection of the plaster originals of his works to the Art Gallery of the University of Michigan at Ann Arbor, Palmer's casts went to the Albany Institute of History and Art. Rinehart left the casts in his Roman studio to the Peabody Institute in Baltimore and directed that the money in his estate should be used to set up a trust fund "for the promotion of a more highly cultivated taste for art."[5] The trustees have used the income to award scholarships to enable young sculptors to study in Rome. Franklin Simmons left his estate to the Art Association in Portland, Maine, where he had known so many generous patrons. All the casts from the studio of Thomas Crawford were deposited by his widow under the care of the Commissioners of Central Park, New York, and for a time they were exhibited in one of the Park buildings. There was some talk at the time of making them the nucleus of a museum of art, but before this plan could be carried into effect the building was partially destroyed by fire, and though the casts are believed to have been rescued their fate is a mystery, mercifully unsolved.

William Wetmore Story was, among all his other accomplishments, a collector of art objects. He gathered about him antique bits from the broken treasures of Rome and old Italian paintings with which to decorate his suite in the Palazzo Barberini, thus assisting, no doubt, in setting a fashion in collecting and decor, which resulted, one feels, in such museumlike mansions as Mrs. Jack Gardner's Venetian Palace on the Fenway in Boston and a plague of more or less palatial bric-a-brac in parlors throughout the country.

Many young sculptors were fortunate enough to find patrons before they found wide fame. Powers and Clevenger both were enabled to start on their journeys to Italy through the generosity of Nicholas Longworth of Cincinnati—one of the earliest of the Mid-Western Medici and next to John Jacob Astor the richest man in the country. Rinehart received financial help from W. T. Walters of Baltimore; Horatio Greenough enjoyed the

[5] W. S. Rusk, *William Henry Rinehart, Sculptor* (1939).

patronage of Robert Gilmore and James Fenimore Cooper. Thomas Crawford would probably have starved to death but for the commission given him by Prince Demidoff. Randolph Rogers' employers, drygoods merchants in New York, financed his first trip to Italy, an investment they never regretted. The Reverend Henry Bellows, while posing for Hiram Powers in 1868, asked him how far he thought a commonplace artist could go towards success and fame through the backing of powerful friends and fortunate circumstances. And Hiram said, "they can do a great deal at a short heat, but, in a long one, only real merit can win. I have known men of mediocre talents to enjoy, for as much as eight years, a factitious reputation, and then fall into contempt . . . [a man has to have] a burning passion for art, to expect success in it."[6]

In the eighteen thirties and forties it was the fate of our young sculptors to be sent off to Italy to study as soon as they exhibited the slightest talent. They moved like automata through a fanciful ritual guaranteed by established English precedent and approved by men of taste to assure success in the art. It was their fate to be caught in a deadly trap of theory — a totally pedestrian imitation of the Greco-Roman antique past as revived by the classic dreams of the archaeologist Wincklemann and the painter Raphael Mengs.

A few of the sculptors made no move to join their brethren in the Romantic exodus to Italy to study in that vast crumbling university of the sculptural arts which was Rome. Of these, Edward Augustus Brackett had practical sense enough to relinquish the making of portrait busts to make a more important contribution in another field. Erastus Dow Palmer made his reputation chiefly by staying home to deflate the fictitious notion that study in Italy was an absolute necessity for success in sculpture. The religious subject matter of many of his works appealed to the pious who would have been scandalized by the pagan idols of those who had been subject to the spell of the neoclassic pantheon in Italy. William Rimmer actually produced something in the way of sculpture, and his few existing works have an interest for us today *as sculpture,* whereas most of the works of his contemporaries seem more like cultural curios. Robert

Ball Hughes, another member of this group of stay-at-homes, was an emigrant from London who frittered away his Royal Academy training making wax portraits and dabbling in the dubious art of pyrography (drawing pictures on shingles with a hot poker) in Dorchester, Massachusetts, without ever seeing the holy city of art. To James W. A. MacDonald the years he spent studying art in St. Louis in the forties took the place of a trip to Rome; besides, his sculptural style was so realistic he never lacked commissions for Civil War monuments — possibly he never had time to get away.

Though every sculptor save Clevenger lived through the world-wide fever and madness of the Gold Rush of '49, not one of them turned his steps westward, California bound.[7] MacDonald came east from St. Louis to study art in New York in '49. Story was in Boston trying to make up his mind whether to be a lawyer or a sculptor. Crawford in that year came from Rome to visit his friends in Bordentown, New Jersey, and dashed off his prize-winning sketch for the Washington Monument in Richmond, Virginia, whereupon he returned to Rome. At the time a number of the men in the group were staying in Italy and apparently the rest, wherever they were, preferred the stones of Carrara to those of the Sierra. Perhaps they were wise in letting someone else dig for gold in the hot canyons of California, for, a few years later, they were able to make traveling bonanza kings "pan out" to the tune of $1,000 a head for portrait busts of their daughters.

Though the Civil War served our sculptors well in loosing a flood of commissions for memorial monuments, very few of the men in the group seem to have been directly involved in the war. Many of them at the time were living permanently in Italy. But if the War had little effect on their lives it had a very great effect on their sculpture. Perhaps the demand for equestrian monuments prompted a new interest in animal sculpture and certainly it gave a new impetus to the already well-developed interest in highly realistic portraiture. The classic toga which enhanced the portrait busts of the forties and fifties was discarded after the war for the faithful representation of military uniforms complete with detailed medals, buttons, epaulette fringes, and other insignia of rank and valor. The genteel interest in the classical past was brought up sharply by the grim reality of immediate events, and older gods were overshadowed by the fame of new heroes. No one ever thought of representing Gen-

---

[6] H. W. Bellows, *Seven Sittings with Powers the Sculptor* (1869).
[7] James B. Dunlap, sculptor, of Indianapolis, went to California sometime in the 1850's in search of health, we are told, and not as a gold miner.

eral Grant as a Roman soldier or even as Mars. Undoubtedly the war had much to do with the change in outlook, which suddenly seemed to make the unrealities of the neo-classic style lose their fascination for both artist and connoisseur.

Most of the sculptors captured the interest of their contemporaries as much by their pleasing personalities as by the romantic fact of being sculptors. Even before William Wetmore Story gave the clan a certain mark of social éclat by his high connections in Boston and Roman society, the sculptors were noted as a class to stand out above the general ruck of artists who merely painted. Hawthorne says "the men of marble appear to have more weight with the public than the men of canvas ... To be a sculptor seems a distinction in itself; whereas a painter is nothing unless individually eminent."[8] The sculptors seemed to move in a glow of specious dignity reflected from the noble marble and their grandiose subject matter.

With only a few exceptions, as we have already noted, the road to wide fame and financial success opened up to our sculptors after they had made their first portrait bust of some prominent political figure. But, next to strong political friends, the best way to sculptural notoriety was the production of a female nude, especially if one could secure a published endorsement from a popular clergyman. In the forties and fifties a nude statue with clerical backing was found to be irresistible.

Others found the way to fame with a timely sculptural group or figure that tied in with the current interests of the day. There was certainly a discernable preoccupation with chains, shackles, and slaves which found expression in American sculpture. Perhaps it was not only the effect of the burning slavery question of the day, perhaps it was symbolic of the sculptors' bondage to materialism and inexperience. In any case this concern with chains amounted almost to a national mania.

During their careers our sculptors gathered many desirable honors. Some of the sculptors were quite happy to be honored with more commissions for portrait busts than they could conveniently execute. Some of them enjoyed (in lieu of academic degrees) medals for "excellence in statuary" awarded by local Mechanics Institutes. Many of them basked in the coveted acclaim of European art critics, connoisseurs, collectors, and art museum curators. Traveling royalty showered them with ribboned jewels. Two American sculptors won the distinction of election as councilors of the Academy of St. Luke in Rome (the oldest art academy in the world) an honor held in succession by Thomas Crawford and Randolph Rogers. During the course of his career Rogers was awarded the insignia of a Cavalliere della Corona d'Italia and William Story also held some order from the Italian court. Henry Kirke Brown served on a commission on fine arts appointed by President Buchanan in 1859, for which he wrote[9] a report designed to make congressmen and senators less gullible in matters of art. But the best honor of all was reserved for that most typical Yankee and hundred-per-cent American, Hiram Powers; *he* had an Ohio River steamer named after him—an indication of the widespread regard in which he was held by his countrymen.

Hiram Powers, John Rogers, William Story, and Harriet Hosmer were all assisted on their way to fame by exhibiting their work at the industrial expositions that were such a feature of the nineteenth century. Expositions have ever since been one of the most important forces in forwarding the art of sculpture. Powers's *Greek Slave* was the peerless sensation of the Great Crystal Palace Exhibition in London in 1851. Story's *Cleopatra* and his *Libyan Sibyl* created a furore at the Exposition of 1862 in London. John Rogers' *Checkers up at the Farm* was the artistic gem of the Cosmopolitan Charity Bazaar in Chicago in 1859. The art exhibition in connection with this event, the first ever held in Chicago, was organized by another American sculptor—Leonard W. Volk.

Though not all of the sculptors were born Yankees, in the strict sense of the term, they were all ingenious, they all had definite mechanical inclinations, and they were all remarkably adaptable. The most consummate Yankee of them all, and the best mechanic too, was Hiram Powers. Though he lived in Florence for thirty-six years without ever returning to the land of his birth, he remained a Vermont man to the core.

Franklin Simmons was a late-comer to the group but he represents the die-hard type, who clung, in the face of a changing world, to the old neoclassic conventions long past their heyday. He did not go to Rome until after the Civil War and he lingered there until his death in 1913. There he sought to recapture the classic phantoms that lurked in the scarcely visible afterglow of the Roman Art

[8] Hawthorne, *The Marble Faun.*

[9] With the assistance of the painters Lambdin and Kensett.

Life glimmering down the century from the far-away past when Canova was in his prime.

At least fifteen of the men in the group died in Europe and some of them were buried in the Protestant cemeteries of Italy to mingle their dust with that of notable English Romantic poets who had come to Italy to sing of Liberty and the Grecian ideal beauty of the "old antique." Seven of them died young, leaving their greatest works unfinished: Clevenger, Crawford, Rinehart, Galt, Barbee, Akers, and Bartholomew.

It would seem that in those days a man could scarcely put hand to clay or take up mallet and chisel without being hailed as a genius whose life was dedicated to high art and the pursuit of ideal beauty. The Art Journals, Drawing Room Companions, and newspapers of the day (including the *Boston Pilot,* a paper with an intense interest in the career of William Story) all encouraged the notion that each work as it issued from the studio was an imperishable masterpiece—whereas perhaps they were really only too imperishable. The few writers who dared to raise their voices to criticize adversely were branded as twisted characters, lacking in patriotism, probable harborers of jealous thoughts.

The sculptors encouraged themselves by a belief that they were "improving" on the Greeks, whose principal faults, in their eyes, were an unfair antique opportunity for studying the nude and a complete lack of the spiritual refinements of Protestant Christianity. One contemporary writer says: "The leading characteristic of the [modern] style is a unity of beauty and dignity which, while it gives to [the] . . . faces the expression of high ideality, still leaves them human, possible, loving. It is as if the old Greeks had become Christianized and *practical*—as if Praxiteles had given his cunning into the keeping of one who sought the avenues of the heart rather than those of the mind."[10]

After studying the works of these men one begins to realize that among the principal reasons for the peculiar qualities of their work were their lack of early training, the classical conventions in which they tried to believe, and also the fact that all their works in marble passed through the facile unfeeling hands of Italian marble workers.

This was one of their greatest misfortunes. It is readily to be seen that such of their works as were cast in bronze do not suffer so much from the careful vacuousness and busyness of surface detail which is, in such large part, the thoughtless virtuosity of skilled stonecutters and marble polishers. The men who stayed at home to work in the United States did not have to add to their own failings those of the commercial Italian tombstone makers.

Jarves reports:

Much of the workmanship so attractive to the untrained eye is the handicraft of artisans. Powers gets the best he can at annual wages of a few hundred dollars each, some of whom have the feeling and knowledge of real artists. Chantrey paid a thousand pounds sterling to his two best cutters, and they made work which was passed for and was paid for as his, in one instance as high as five hundred pounds sterling for a repetition of a bust of George IV for the Duke of Devonshire. . . . We mention these facts, that those who attach so much importance to the mere workmanship of the American school may learn that even in that quality it is not beyond indebtedness to foreign sources.[11]

Another characteristic of the sculpture of the time which we find annoying is the look of sameness—an impersonal quality in the works of entirely different men as though they had all been done by the same hand. There is a monotony of surface—which Jarves likened to ivory-turning—in all these marbles. We may be sure that the great leveler and polisher was none other than the professional marble-worker. In the busy studios of American sculptors the Carrara blocks were pulverized under the hands of Italian artisans whose familiarity with marble seemed to produce a cold contempt for the material, which they belabored and abraded with a truly monstrous facility.

Hawthorne, visiting Roman studios, remarked upon the superiority of the clay models to the finished products in marble but everyone else in his day seemed overcome by the virtues attributed by literary sentimentalists to the artist's materials. Clay was common, dull, pliable, dirty, impermanent; marble was "white moonlight," imperishable, immortal, casting an antiseptic moral air over any subject represented—rendering even female nudity acceptable in a morbidly squeamish age.

The Italian marble-workers were not wholly to blame for the adenoidal vacancy which the sculptors of the neoclassic school mistook for an expression of sublimity. The sculptors, through constant study and a completely uncritical acceptance of all the Greek and Roman sculpture

---

[10] *Cosmopolitan Art Journal,* IV (Dec. 1860).

[11] *Art Idea* (1864).

they found in the galleries of Rome, both good and bad, pieced together their "creations" by stealing a head here, a torso there, bits of drapery and stage props from another antique statue or relief. Indeed, one of the reasons they loved Rome so well was because of its endless ranks of antique marbles which made it such an inexhaustible mine of ready-made sculptural "ideas" from which to assemble their masterpieces.

Hawthorne, speaking through the lips of one of his characters in *The Marble Faun,* says:

The difficulty goes to confirm me in my belief that, except for portrait busts, sculpture has no longer a right to claim any place among the living arts. It has wrought itself out, and come fairly to an end. There is never a new group nowadays, never so much as a new attitude. Greenough (I take my examples among men of merit) imagined nothing new; Crawford either, except in the tailoring line. There are not, as you will own, more than half a dozen original statues or groups in the world, and these few are of immemorial antiquity. A person familiar with the Vatican, the Uffizi Gallery, the Naples Gallery, and the Louvre, will at once refer any modern production to its antique prototype, which, moreover, had begun to get out of fashion, even in old Roman days. . . . Fairly own to me, then, my friend . . . that you sculptors are of necessity, the greatest plagiarists in the world.

To the close student of classical sculpture their works appear to be little more than syncretic monstrosities composed of recognizable fragments from the less publicized artistic remains of Greece and Rome. Here, for instance, among the works of William Story, is *Medea,* a draped standing figure "lifted" from a Pompeian fresco, its head, however, stolen from a masculine portrait bust of a different period. A curious feather headdress, something like those seen in seventeenth century engravings of American Indians, quickly turns a classical Amazon into a *Mexican Princess* (the work of Thomas Crawford), and a toga draped in the Flavian mode transforms an American Quaker gentleman into a Roman statesman.

"Plagiarism," says Jarves, "is rife among some of our artists, because of their indifference to the requirements of high art and unwillingness to acknowledge their obligations to others. . . . We have Pandoras, Ganymedes, Cupids, and other similar feeble reproductions of classical sculpture in scores."[12]

The less skillful sculptors merely "borrowed" gestures and trappings, but Powers's greater technical dexterity

[12] *Art Idea.*

and his gang of expert workmen enabled him to steal surface textures as well. He was noted for his ability to give his figures a soft Praxitelean texture that left his contemporaries gasping with awe. It was one of his boasts that he had himself invented tools with which to accomplish this miracle. He often thought seriously of patenting the process. Signor Migliarini, the curator of the Grand Ducal Gallery in Florence, was completely captivated by our Grecian genius from Vermont and called him "the first sculptor of the age."

With few exceptions, the sculptors seem to have attained a dead level of plastic ineptitude which was so obvious that even the well-intentioned critics of their time were finally forced to mention it. However, above this monotonous desert prairie certain stones are raised by an approach to true sculptural quality. Somehow it managed to creep into a few of their works, transcending the bonds of contemporary convention. These mild eminences are, of course, widely scattered on the plain —one is only surprised, considering the nature of the terrain, that there are any eminences at all. Highest among these eminences rise the extraordinary works by that rarest, and by modern standards best, American sculptor of the period, Dr. William Rimmer. Perhaps he should not even be considered as a member of our happy band of self-exiled Yankee stonecutters. He alone is here in the group (a sculptor surrounded by mechanics) merely by accident of the date of his birth. Beside him the other sculptors take their places as little more than portrait machines. Unfortunately only about a half dozen of his sculptural works remain in existence today. He stands alone on the periphery of the Yankee art world, a lonely mysterious figure. The other men all follow a definite "period pattern" in their lives and works. They furnish the background of mediocrity before which, in monumental contrast, Rimmer stands as a creative giant.

The works of John Rogers, who was for many years an actual engineer and mechanic before he took up the art of sculpture as a life work, are worthy of being singled out because they preserve so charmingly certain vanished phases of American life that were quite ignored by his classically minded fellows. Palmer is noteworthy because he had the intelligence to stay at home. Rinehart, who had excellent opportunities to know his tools and materials, was trapped like the rest by the demands of his patrons and by his commonplace imagination. Powers, with the right kind of an education, would, undoubtedly, have been an inventor as valued as Morse or McCormick or Blanchard.

As the century progressed, evidences of the waning power of the neoclassic doctrines become more and more obvious in the works of the men in the group. They were overwhelmed in the rising tides of realism until finally the white marble itself remained as almost the only concession to what were rapidly becoming old-fashioned notions. Naturally, the break from neoclassicism is first to be seen in the works of the men who did not go to Italy[13] or those who, going, stayed only a short time.[14] The Greco-Roman spell reached them principally through books and engravings, often badly redrawn, or filtered through plaster casts and the works of other American sculptors. The artists scarcely noticed their departure from classic models.

To those who cherish the notions of their grandparents, white marble is still the paramount requisite for sculpture. The taste for sculpture so carefully nurtured in the 19th century, and the standards then established still have an undeniable power among the uncritical—a fact too often overlooked by those who run at the front of the van of new movements in the world of art. As against the few who lead the way to new fields, there remains the great mass stalled in the green pastures of yesterday, blissfully unaware of the skipping will-o'-the-wisp of aesthetic fashions and the seductive theories of professors.

After the middle of the nineteenth century, with the gradual shifting of the center of the art world from Rome to Paris, the works of the earlier men were dismissed as outmoded and bad by the artists of the younger generation. The flow of adverse criticism begins to rise about 1860 and increases thereafter. Though many of the older men continued to live in Italy and to work in the old traditions, all their fine white marbles, which had seemed to pre-Civil War connoisseurs so like, yet so superior to the antique, were cast aside in favor of the increasingly naturalistic bronzes made by sculptors trained in the ateliers of Paris. The Centennial Exposition in Philadelphia in 1876 furnished the stage for the last public appearance of our early melodramatists in marble in the role of geniuses. From that time forward the Italo-Yankee school faded rapidly away into the green-velour dimness of provincial parlours and the lumber rooms of second-string auction houses. The new men took the stage and held it—the World's Columbian Exposition in Chicago in 1893 was all theirs. They peopled a world with bronzes of caramel gentility, which are, at the moment, as passé as the works of the neoclassic men they displaced in popular favor. The new men, the younger generation of 1870–80, became the geniuses of the hour.

In early days, by nature taught
  The love her works impart,
He had from dreamy musings woke
  To woo the plastic art
With wondrous skill, life's varied forms
  Grew fair beneath his hand,
And he had lived with joy to see
  Their beauty fill the land.[15]

[15] From a poem entitled "The Group; a Christmas Ballad," by Edward Augustus Brackett, read at the anniversary of the Eurosophian Adelphi at Waterville College, August 2, 1845. Published in *My House, Chips the Builder Threw Away*, a volume of poems by E. A. Brackett (New York, 1904).

[13] For example, Rimmer, Palmer, MacDonald, Ball Hughes, Brackett.
[14] For example, Brown, John Rogers, Volk.

4 · CLAY FIGURES
or, Some Representative Men

There is no statue like this living man, with his infinite advantage over all ideal sculpture, of perpetual variety. What a gallery of art have I here! No mannerist made these varied groups and diverse original figures. Here is the artist himself improvising grim and glad, at his block ... Away with your nonsense of oil and easels, of marble and chisels; except to open your eyes to the masteries of eternal art, they are hypocritical rubbish.

RALPH WALDO EMERSON

Thomas Crawford: The Grecian Genius

IN the eighteen forties and fifties the circumstances of the time required the appearance of a great American genius of sculpture. There was an apparently irrepressible yearning for some native American to rival at least the glory of Canova and Thorwaldsen, if not of Phidias. The many admirers of the sculptor Thomas Crawford sought this honor for him. They regarded his talent through a romantic haze of wishful thinking that was strongly colored by national pride. Perhaps Crawford the sculptor should be considered as the result of social phenomena in his environment rather than as a creative artist. Time has proven that his friends were unfortunately hasty, not to say somewhat undignified, in their eagerness to establish him as the leading genius of a national culture-legend. In the accounts of Crawford's career and character we find embalmed the hero worship of a generation starving for an art idol in the realm of sculpture. They seemed to find something peculiarly rewarding in the admiration of such a curious figure as a financially successful sculptor.

Of all his claims to fame, that which most often impressed his friends was the simple fact of his American birth. To them he presaged the dawn of a new golden age of art in the New World. Charles Sumner refers to the young Crawford, saying, "The star of Art perhaps, shall follow that of Empire in its westward way. Already we see and bless its mild effulgence."[16] Another friend writes, "He will be the first of *modern* sculptors; nay, an American may rival Phidias ..."[17] Other writers let themselves run on in resounding phrases of unreserved praise in which Crawford was always linked with the bright dawn of a new era. In 1855 a correspondent of the London *Art Journal,* writing from Rome under the pen name of Fiorentina, reports, "There is a great artistic movement taking place in the great continent. Americans are great travellers: ... they are enlightened and prodigal patrons of Art and artists ... they ... would deck their virgin soil with the finest productions of native genius—an easy task while they possess artists like Crawford..."[18] Later the *American Quarterly Church Review and Ecclesiastical Register* records, "A number of works intended to ornament the Capitol at Washington were committed to Crawford—a national recognition of his genius. There was a feeling among us ... that the time was come, the golden hour arrived, when the character of American art was to be redeemed; when the chosen sculptor of the nation was to achieve works worthy of comparison with the greatest works of ancient or of modern sculpture; when the country was to be rescued from her dependence on foreign artists, and to rejoice in a Phidias of her own. . ."[19] Seldom has so slender a talent for modeling won for an artist so much unqualified acclaim as in the case of Thomas Crawford.

One searches for the man himself beneath the excessive verbiage of his admirers. To them he fulfilled every requisite of their prescription for genius. He had risen by hard work from humble circumstances to the social éclat of a matrimonial union with the daughter of a New York banker. His complete absorption and joy in the work of the studio delighted them as something quite extraordinary. His happy home life was contrasted with "the riot and excess of that wild life in which so many Artists waste their time and impair their powers." It seemed to them fitting that a genius "found little satisfaction in the light pleasures of society."[20] They erected around the sturdy armature of his essentially simple personality an elaborate romantic structure of impossible virtues, clothing a lay figure of artistic mediocrity in the heavy cloak of genius.

[16] C. Sumner, "Crawford's Orpheus," *United States Magazine and Democratic Review* (May 1843).
[17] *Ibid.*
[18] *Art Journal,* XVII (1855).
[19] *American Quarterly Church Review* (April, 1858).
[20] *Ibid.*

Crawford's most influential friend was the lawyer Charles Sumner (later United States senator from Massachusetts), a brilliant and highly cultivated Bostonian whose forensic displays on the lecture platform made him a powerful figure in political and cultural circles both in England and in America. Thomas Crawford's wife, Louisa, a member of the celebrated Ward family of New York, was a strong-minded and persistent lady, determined that her husband should be a financial success as well as a genius.

Those who were not exposed to the charm of Crawford's personality and were impervious to the genius-legend so carefully engineered by his friends and family, could look at his sculptured works with much the same objectivity we have toward them today. Hawthorne, who visited Crawford's studio shortly after the sculptor's death in 1857, was very little impressed with what he saw there. The famous Richmond Washington monument seemed to him to be "merely an ingenious contrivance" though he admits it "will produce a moral effect." Crawford's other works, he criticizes without mercy as "commonplaces in marble and plaster such as we would not tolerate on a printed page."[21] Even such a notably generous critic as Lorado Taft can find little to praise in the work of our poor Grecian Genius.

Though Crawford was not by any means the first American artist to visit Rome, he is believed to have been the first American sculptor to go there for the purpose of studying sculpture. He was welcomed into the studio of Thorvaldsen, where he received some instruction from that master. Soon after his arrival in Rome, Crawford wrote to his friend Robert Launitz, the New York tombstone carver, "You can imagine my surprise upon seeing the wonderful halls of the Vatican—after leaving Barclay Street[22] and the National.[23] Only think of it—a green one like me, who had seen but a half dozen statues during the whole course of his life—to step thus suddenly into the midst of the greatest collection in the world!"[24]

It is a commentary on the teaching methods of the National Academy of Design, where Crawford studied before going to Rome, to find that he was still making the beginner's error of fussing endlessly with niggling details and finish when he arrived at the studio of Thor-

valdsen. One of the first lessons that Thorvaldsen taught him was to consider the larger aspects of his work, the masses and volumes of sculpture and the principal actions, and to leave the details until he had mastered the art of blocking things in "in the large." This commonplace bit of advice seemed to the young sculptor a most wonderful revelation and he often remarked upon it as the real beginning of his understanding of the plastic art, the source of his great debt to Thorvaldsen.

Everyone was impressed with the speed and endless variety of Crawford's creative genius—it is said that above his studio he kept a room full of small clay sketches of sculptural ideas that had come to him while he was working on his larger projects. The flow of his ideas was of such force and insistence that he often had to stop work on his monuments to dash off these little models. Sculptural ideas seemed "to rise spontaneously and intuitively at Crawford's bidding. He hit off his marble epics as a poet would turn a graceful stanza. . ."[25]

Regarding one of these creations the sculptor writes (1843): "I have commenced a small statue of youth, for Mr. Hicks, of New York. The model will be completed in about a month. It is a boy of seven or eight years, dancing in great glee, and tinkling a pair of cymbals, the music of which seems to amuse him exceedingly. The sentiment is joyousness throughout. It is evident no thought of the future troubles his young mind: and he may consider himself very fortunate in being made of marble; for thus his youth remains without change. . ."
A correspondent of the New York *Evening Post,* writing of this figure, says:

Here, in Rome, I have frequently seen Crawford, a native of New York; after struggling against many difficulties he has now won a proud reputation. . . . Crawford's rising fame has lately brought him several orders, and he is now in a fair way of overcoming all the obstacles that impeded him in his earliest career. He has just completed a very fine figure, which he calls The Genius of Mirth. Henry W. Hicks, Esq., of New-York, who was here some time ago, pleased with Crawford's genius, and desirous of encouraging him, gave him an unconditional order, at a liberal price . . . the Artist has exhibited much taste in the selection of the subject. The Genius of Mirth, is truly a clever work—it is finished, and has been sent to Leghorn for shipment.

It is unnecessary to describe this figure—you will doubtless see it soon, then, judge for yourself, if my estimate of Crawford's merit is too high.

[21] Hawthorne, *Passages from the French and Italian Note-Books.*
[22] That is, The American Academy of Fine Arts.
[23] That is, The National Academy of Design.
[24] R. E. Launitz, "Reminiscences of Thomas Crawford," *Crayon,* VI (1859).

[25] *Art Journal,* XVII (1855).

"By the way, as you know Mr. Hicks, I wish you would whisper in his ear, to send the Genius of Mirth to the first exhibition of the Academy—justice to the sculptor, not less than gratification of his numerous friends, should persuade him to do so..."[26]

By a curious coincidence, while Crawford was engrossed in making sculpture that has practically nothing to do with form, his brother-in-law, Sam Ward, a literary amateur, coined the now familiar phrase "significant form" for a paper he wrote on "Criticism."[27]

Crawford's monumental works received much special attention. He could scarcely finish them before the studio was swarming with visitors—when the Washington monument was finished in plaster so many enthusiastic admirers were attracted to the studio they could be admitted on only one day of the week in order that the normal work of the studio might go forward. When this monument was cast in bronze at the Royal Foundry in Munich, the foundry workers held a little celebration of their own in honor of the patriot Washington and the artist Crawford. The successful casting of Crawford's Beethoven, commissioned by Charles Perkins for the Music Hall in Boston, was the occasion of a special musical festival in Munich with the statue holding the central place of honor upon the concert stage. When it was unveiled in Boston, another elaborate ceremony took place which included a dedicatory poem composed by the sculptor William Wetmore Story. Naturally, when the colossal Armed Freedom was hoisted to its pedestal, an honorary booming of cannon marked the event.

Perhaps no piece of sculpture executed by an American artist enjoys so conspicuous and important a situation—indeed, with the passing of the years, the pedestal has grown so important that today the figure of Armed Freedom suffers an almost total eclipse. It has become so much a part of its surroundings as to be practically invisible. This is probably its greatest virtue as sculpture. Today it is often mistaken for an Indian Warrior, or Liberty, or Miss Columbia—few know its correct title and fewer still remember the name of the sculptor.

The pedestal which has thus overshadowed its sculptured burden is the Capitol in Washington—Armed Freedom caps the dome. Certainly no monument in the United States can rival the importance of its location—though many enjoy an equally conspicuous oblivion.

The dramatic circumstances of Crawford's death from a brain cancer at the height of his career contributed much to his fame and gave his emotional contemporaries an opportunity for funeral orations and eulogies that they did not fail to improve. Henry Tuckerman wrote a long dirge of "exquisitely sympathetic verses" on "The Funeral of Thomas Crawford." George Hillard, the Boston lawyer, and Thomas Hicks, the New York artist, both prepared eulogies which were half obituary and half art lecture. In these and other similar works published at the time of his death, Crawford the sculptor appears as the culminating genius at the apex of the slow pyramid of recorded time. Crawford the man emerges from their perfervid oratory with a character of lofty nobility and unblemished manly beauty. Though the laurels of his crown of genius have long since withered, time cannot rob him of the many deserved tributes to his fine personal character. Today we may tender to his memory a floral offering of daisy, sage, and sweetbrier, the flower symbols of Naïvete, Domestic Virtue, and Simplicity.

In Fortune's noon of might
Came the relentless blight,
And Life's best triumphs thou no more could share;
Those hands that nobly wrought,
And truth enamoured sought,
The chisel loosened then—to fold in prayer!
The Grief whose shadows rest
Here in thy native West,
An echo wakes in Art's perennial clime;
Thy marble children wait,
In beauty desolate,
And brothers mourn thee in the haunt of Time![28]

Hiram Powers: The Sublime Mechanic

HIRAM POWERS was scarce laid in his grave in the Protestant cemetery in Florence[29] when people began to remark on how much beautiful white marble had been spoiled by the sculptors of the Yankee school of which Hiram was the most widely renowned member. Though few people remember him today, he was in his time, without exception, the most famous American artist both at home and abroad. Among his friends and patrons were numbered some of the most accomplished literary men of the

---

[26] C. Edwards Lester, The Artists of America (1845). N.B.: This figure is now in the Metropolitan Museum of Art.
[27] Published in Aesthetic Papers, 1849 (a periodical).

[28] Henry T. Tuckerman, "The Funeral of Thomas Crawford," in Book of the Artists.
[29] 1873.

century and many of the men of great wealth. His sculptured works found favored places in the manor houses of the English nobility, the palaces of Russian princes, and in the elaborate Gothic mansions of prairie millionaires and real-estate kings in New York.

He was noted in his day as a conversationalist and has left for us in his talk a most entertaining picture of himself, his ideas on art, and his times. Among these recorded conversations we find an interesting contrast, in the following accounts, of the impression he made. The Reverend Henry Bellows accepted the man at his face value:

Florence, Italy, May 1, 1868. Four P. M.—I have just returned to my lodgings from my first sitting to Hiram Powers, and he has interested me so much by his conversation while at work, that it occurs to me that I can hardly do a better service to Art than to jot down freshly, from day to day, the more striking things that fall from his lips—specially in relation to his art, in which he is so acknowledged a master.[30]

Nathaniel Hawthorne looked at Hiram a little more critically:

I have hardly ever before felt an impulse to write down a man's conversation as I do that of Mr. Powers. The chief reason is, probably, that it is so possible to do it, his ideas being square solid, and tangible, and therefore readily grasped and retained. He is a very instructive man, and sweeps one's empty and dead notions out of the way with exceeding vigour; but when you have his ultimate thought and perception, you feel inclined to think and see a little further for yourself. He sees too clearly what is within his range to be aware of any region of mystery beyond.[31]

Very few men indeed have the power to send their contemporaries rushing for pen and paper to record their conversations, but Hiram Powers seems to have affected a number of people in this fashion. He must indeed have been a remarkable man—a "character"—we should say.

Let us return to the Reverend Henry Bellows for another look at Hiram:

If I were to give my own picture of the artist in an off-hand way. . . . I should speak somewhat thus:

Mr. Powers has the distinguishing mark of intellectual greatness . . . he is able to grasp principles without forgetting details. . . . He is the closest observer of special facts. This self-centered quality accounts for the persistency of the original simplicity and American type of his character and genius. Thirty years away from home have not affected his patriotism or his New England homeliness. He is every inch an Ameri-

can, and perpetual converse with other nationalities and with all schools of art, has not shaken him from his native style, or the well-considered and home-brewed notions of his vocation that he brought abroad with him . . . [he is] thoroughly unartificialized. . . . Precision is the most marked characteristic of his mind, his eye, his hand. . . .[32]

Obviously he captivated his listeners with his genial talk and a Yankee twang that was piously preserved in his speech—it was one of his most valuable assets in dealing with successful businessmen who have always been inclined to be suspicious of artists. But they could understand Hiram, especially when he kept raising his prices until he could demand and get a thousand dollars for a portrait bust. Powers explained his meager output of "ideal" figures by saying, "For busts I have as many orders as I can execute . . . I must not risk this lucrative business to indulge myself in the works of the imagination." Everyone found him fascinating except the other sculptors, who jealously accused him of being mercenary and limited.

The English art critics and even some of the older artists were most generous in their remarks about Powers. Thorvaldsen declared "The entrance of Powers upon the field constituted an era in art." In the London *Art Journal* for 1841 we find the following: "I had not met Powers previous to visiting his studio, and a finer face it is not possible to conceive, or one more overflowing with genius and imagination. There is an almost superhuman luster in his eyes which gives one an idea that they in themselves contain a creative power, and that he could look a soul into the images he forms. His nudes would not have a tendency to introduce among our women *foreign indelicacy*. . . To other writers "he rivalled the Grace and Beauty of Grecian Genius. . ."

Hawthorne records a number of Powers's conversations, and they range through an extraordinary variety of subjects. Powers had a plan for laying the trans-Atlantic cable that would beat Cyrus Field all hollow, and at his own game too; he airily predicts that flying machines are a certainty of the near future "but not until the moral condition of mankind is so improved as to obviate the bad uses to which the power might be applied"; he recommends cures for burns and complaints of the chest; he demonstrates conclusively that the ancient Greek sculptor who made the Venus di Medici did not know much about anatomy; he compares the musical tones of

[30] Henry W. Bellows, *Seven Sittings with Powers the Sculptor* (1869).
[31] *Passages from the French and Italian Note-Books* (1899).

[32] Bellows, *Seven Sittings.*

the bells of Florence; he talks of Swedenborg, of inhabited planets, and spiritualism; he thinks Michael Angelo a trickster; Canova knew nothing about Nature —his brother sculptors he dismisses with harsh judgments—the German sculptor Schwanthaler he accuses of being a mere *machine* for the production of statues and busts!

Powers's good opinion of his own works and his readiness to answer all questions and solve problems of the most diverse nature give one the impression that he thought he "knew all the answers." It is easy to imagine him well hated by all the other Yankee sculptors in Italy. Hawthorne, though ensnared in the charm of Powers's personality, was enough of a Yankee himself not to be taken in. He accepted Powers's glib statements with a grain of salt. The day after Powers had shown Hawthorne what was wrong with the Venus di Medici, Hawthorne went to see the statue for himself and made his own judgment.

The exhibition of his *Greek Slave* at the Great Crystal Palace Exhibition in London in 1851 spread Powers's renown all over the world. It was the artistic sensation of the age. It was made up of a sure-fire combination of qualities with publicity value; it was nude in a time of excessive feminine upholstery; it was politically timely in title; it was carved from a single block of purest Carrara; it was by an artist, unknown in England, from the supposed cultural desert of America; it had been purchased by a duke of the realm; Queen Victoria and the Prince Consort admired it; Elizabeth Barrett Browning wrote a sonnet about it; the clergy rhapsodized from the pulpit on the subject; it was a success. Hiram made and sold six replicas of the *Slave*—all at prices averaging about $4,000.

Although Hiram spent the most important early years of his artistic life as chief inventor of automata and wax effigies in the Western Museum at Cincinnati, it is interesting to note that the more refined type of biographers and art writers were inclined to suppress this vital fact, as though Powers the waxworker had nothing to do with Powers the sculptor. From the time he was twenty-four until he was in his thirties he worked at the Museum. Before this he had been employed in Watson's clock factory where he demonstrated with clock work the skill which was to come in so handy later at the Museum.

It was due almost entirely to Hiram's ingenuity that the Western Museum was such a financial success. Pos-

sibly the scientific specimens and art curios had some interest for the museum-going public of that day, but what really brought in the crowds was a waxworks chamber of horrors euphemistically termed, among the genteel, "The Regions" or "The Infernal Regions"—a life-size model of Hell. Mrs. Trollope claimed the credit of suggesting to Powers the idea of modeling his show on the descriptions from Dante's Inferno. Apparently the sculptor was inspired, for he invented all sorts of automatic contrivances that groaned and emitted smoke and rattled chains to add a note of realism to the scene. Many lady visitors, too tightly laced for such breath-taking frights, quite swooned away. And the gentlemen tried to maintain a manly calm in the face of an electrical contraption that gave off mysterious shocks and sparks. In the estimation of the local populace for miles around, a trip to Dorfeuille's Hell was almost as refreshing as a good rousing revival meeting, and no trip to the metropolis was complete without a tour of the "Regions." It was here that Powers gained the greater part of his training as a sculptor and doubtless no small part of his knack for selecting sculptural subjects with a popular appeal. It was here that he discovered his ability to "seize a likeness" which later made his marble portraits so valued for their absolute faithfulness.

Leaving Dorfeuille's "Hell" for finer things, Powers set out for Italy, stopping at Washington on the way. Here he was lucky enough to have the hero President —General Jackson—pose for him at the White House. Fortunately a detailed report of Powers's encounter with President Jackson has been preserved—taken down almost word for word from the lips of the sculptor by C. Edwards Lester. From this point we can let Mr. Powers speak for himself. The occasion was to be, throughout Powers's career, a treasured memory and an anecdote often repeated with varying embellishments and improvements for the entertainment of dozing tycoons who, seeking marble immortality, ascended the model's dais in his Florentine studio.

[I] reached Washington just before Congress met in 1835, taking with me letters of introduction to several distinguished gentlemen.

I did not expect any commissions immediately. All I hoped for was to obtain a reputation as an artist; and I began with a bust of General Jackson, who consented in the kindest manner to sit. He took the precaution, however, first of all, to ask me if it was my practice to put plaster on the face to get an impression of the features. On my replying in the negative. he said he was very glad, for he had heard of the manner in which Mr. Jefferson had been taken by Mr. Browere. "And for my part," said he, "I should not like to be tortured or have my ears pulled off, as was the case with that great man when he was obliged to go through that dreadful process."

He showed me an apartment next to his sitting-room, where he said I might arrange my materials. In two days my clay was prepared. The old General entered and going to a shelf at one end of the room he took down a longtailed pipe from one box, and charged it with cut tobacco from another. Pipe in order, he took his seat, and remained with me for about an hour, and during most of the time he smoked and said but little. He was sitting before a window which fronted the Capitol, and I noticed he took off his spectacles and held them some distance from his face and looked some time in the direction of Capitol Hill. At last with an expression of impatience he exclaimed:

"I thought so!—Boys, Mr. Powers, boys!—they are going to have a holiday."

I did not understand this, and perceiving it, he pointed to a flagstaff on the Capitol.

"Don't you see," said he, "the flag is down. They have adjourned over till Tuesday or Wednesday. Congress has just met. That's the way they do. They are all leisure now, and they neglect the public business; but you'll find when the session is drawing to a close all will be hurry and confusion, and Congress will break up leaving much important business undone."

He then knocked the ashes out of his pipe, and laying it on the mantle-piece, he wished me good-day, without taking the slightest notice of my work. I was glad for this for I had yet done but little, and certainly in its then state it had no very promising appearance.

The next day he was engaged, and could not come. "It was not intentional, Mr. Powers," he remarked, "but business prevented me from coming. I'm very sorry for I know your time is precious."

I was deeply struck with this remark; for how true it is, that none but men who have made the most of their time know what time is worth!

Again he charged his pipe, and smoked till he almost fell asleep not-withstanding frequent efforts to rally himself. He appeared exhausted, but he would have sat the whole time, I doubt not, had I not told him I could proceed without him.

"I'm glad," he replied, "for I am not well today, but I will try to sit better for you tomorrow."

The day following, as he laid down his pipe on the mantle-piece as he was leaving, I asked him if he would give me the pipe he had been using. It was a common clay pipe, although it would have been esteemed a Jackson pipe, perhaps.

"Why, Mr. Powers," said he with a smile, "it is a valueless thing, and not worth your taking; but I have a very beautiful pipe in the other room, made by an Indian, and I would give it to you with great satisfaction if you would take it."

I replied that it was not the Indian's pipe, but General Jackson's pipe I wanted.

"Ah, well, Sir," he replied with a laugh, "you shall have it with all my heart." He then took it from the mantle-piece, and stepping forward, presented it to me with all that dignity and elegant courtesy of manner, of which he was so perfect a master when the occasion called for it.

Just before I finished the bust Major Donaldson [Donelson] paid me a visit, as he had done often before during the progress of the work, and he remarked that perhaps I had copied the peculiarities of the mouth too faithfully; alleging that the General had lost his teeth, or rather, laid them aside, and that his mouth had fallen in, which left him, in that respect, unlike his former self. But I liked the expression of his mouth, even as it was; for it's a remarkable fact, that when nature is defeated by age, accident or infirmity, of her original design, she will still find some means of reproducing it, and such is particularly the case with General Jackson. The same firmness and inflexibility of character his mouth expressed in the prime of life, is to be found there still, though the forms are entirely changed. It is an error to suppose that features are accidental, and nature makes them up at hap-hazard; for the face is the true index of the soul, *where everything is written had we the wisdom to read it.* . . .

The suggestion of Major Donaldson was kind, but I did not think it advisable to act upon it. I determined however to mention it to General Jackson, and ascertain what he thought about it.

"Make me as I am, Mr. Powers," he replied, "and be true to nature always, and in everything. It's the only safe rule to follow. I have no desire to *look* young as long as I *feel* old: and then it seems to me, although I don't know much about sculpture, that the only object in making a bust is to get a representation of the man who sits, that it be as nearly as possible a perfect likeness. If he has no teeth why then make him *with* teeth?"

This was his last sitting, and he stood before the bust and examined it for the first time.

"But after all I've said," he continued, "of course I'm no judge, I don't profess to understand these things — I can't judge either, perhaps, so well of my own likeness as I could of another's. But Colonel Earl [the portrait painter] can tell you more about it, and I advise you to get him to look at it."

He then bade me adieu, wishing me every success with my *picture* [sic].

I have never had a more striking subject for a bust than General Jackson; and I doubt if the whole range of subjects would furnish another like it.[33]

After Powers settled in Italy he proceeded to copy his clay bust of Jackson in white marble. Mr. Miner K.

[33] C. E. Lester, *The Artist.* For further details regarding this bust, see Metropolitan Museum of Art, *Bulletin,* N.S. II, No. 2, Oct., 1943.

Kellogg, Powers' agent, who at one time owned the Jackson bust, believed this to be the only marble bust carved in the stone entirely by Hiram Powers' own hand. However, the sculptor himself says, according to Bellows: "I found labor cheap enough [in Italy], but laborers, used to or capable of reproducing my kind of modelling, absolutely unobtainable. After trying many, I had to go to work and cut four of the busts with my own hands, at a ruinous cost of time and money." In all probability Jackson's bust was one of these four. Shortly after this, fortunately for him, Powers discovered a competent but unsuccessful sculptor who became the chief workman of his studio, remaining with him for over thirty years.

Most of the art critics ran through their entire gamut of superlatives when they wrote of the man and his sculpture. To them even genius seemed too feeble a word to support the grandeur of their claims for him. The sculptural monuments of the Classical past and the Renaissance became mere stones again and on top of the pile stood the paragon Powers. They said:

It is only just to add that no modern artist has better understood this secret of power than our countryman Powers. The austere genius of Buonarotti, who dashed out his most superb conceptions in marble, with an impatient hand, sacrificed beauty to expression, so that in fidelity and exquisite finish our sculptor surpasses him.[34]

And again:

In reference to Mr. Powers' statues . . . they even represent the *porosities* of the skin—a perfection which seems incredible. It is accounted for by the fact that the eminent sculptor is also a very ingenious mechanician, and has invented an almost entire new set of tools, far superior to those used in sculpture from time immemorial. One of these instruments imparts to the surface of the marble a delicate "roughness," which so perfectly counterfeits the porosities and wrinkles of the skin as to produce the impression of excessive and minute labor.[35]

Rare and unwelcome was the critic who could write of Powers:

He defied all conventionalism, and represented just what he saw without reference to the canons of "classical" art. But, he is a pure actualist; his work is all surface; and, beyond that point, he had not the ability to pass. The history of criticism presents no stranger thing than the reputation of his "Greek Slave." It was owing primarily to English critics, who, as a class, are the very weakest authority in matters of art. In fact,

beyond a marvelous rendering of the mere flesh qualities, there is not one excellence to recommend it . . . its anatomical faults are so numerous it would be easier to say what is right than what is wrong. It has no central idea save that of nudity . . . and, all the false sentiment of fanciful sonneteers and commentators has only had the effect to disguise from the public the real nature of the statue, more lascivious than anything Greek art has left to us, without its redeeming technical excellence.[36]

It was a wonder that such a criticism could find a publisher in 1860. The editor of the *Cosmopolitan Art Journal* hastily disclaims any concurrence with the views of the author and offers it to his readers as an example of what curious and wrong-headed ideas some people may have.

As an artist Powers is of interest today merely as a faithful recorder of historic shapes—the portrait busts of prominent figures of his time. He typifies the "ingenious Yankee mechanic," by being more ingenious, more Yankee, and more mechanical than any of the rest of the sculptors of the neoclassic group. A Boston critic dubbed him "the sublime mechanic." He was adaptable, simple, shrewd, crafty, and limited. Powers' agent, Miner K. Kellogg, had good reason to know the lengths to which the Vermont genius could carry his shrewdness. Mr. Kellogg claims that not only did he loan money to Powers in the lean days when he arrived in Florence but that he also financed and managed the exhibition tour of the *Greek Slave* in the United States, a show which grossed the astonishing sum of $23,500. When the time came to settle accounts, the sculptor was very slow and finally Kellogg had to threaten suit to collect his due. Powers was unwilling to close the matter until he had examined Kellogg's books and papers. Mr. Kellogg, in good faith, took his records to Powers and left them with him—a fatal mistake. The sculptor refused to return Mr. Kellogg's papers because, as he admitted, before witnesses, "he did not wish a paper to get before the world in which he acknowledged his indebtedness for his success in any way to Mr. Kellogg."

The threat of a law suit over this matter and the adverse publicity which that would entail were factors which prevented Powers from ever returning to the United States but more important as a deterrent to travel was his absolute dependence on his crew of Italian marble-workers.

He had the brash assurance of the man of small intel-

[34] *Cosmopolitan Art Journal*, I (Nov., 1856), 56.
[35] *Ibid.*, II (Dec., 1857), 33.

[36] *Ibid.*, IV (Mar., 1860).

lectual powers. Everywhere that he is mentioned one sees the word "straightforward." To his contemporaries not the least appealing characteristic of the man was his financial success and the piquant rags-to-riches element of dramatic contrast in his "self-made" career.

Those who knew him best said that, had he not discovered that he was born to be an artist he would have been one of the world's greatest inventors.

Erastus Dow Palmer: The Inspired Carpenter

THAT the flight to foreign shores was almost pure romance, and really quite unnecessary for "success in the sculptorial art," would probably not have occurred to many American sculptors save for the extraordinary career of Erastus Dow Palmer. He found beauty and fame awaiting him in the shadow of the State Capitol in Albany. With no instruction in art, with no classical sculpture convenient for copying, with scarcely any education to speak of, without the potent glamour of a residence in Rome, he became a leading figure in the American art world of his time and a sculptor whose work today stands somewhat above that of most of his contemporaries. All this he accomplished by staying at home and industriously applying to sculpture the craftsman's training which he had gained as a master carpenter and builder before he took up the art.

Palmer showed his manual skill while he was still quite young—it is said that he was, even as a boy of twelve, a very good carpenter—and he soon progressed to building houses and designing the more complicated architectural features, such as staircases and paneling. As a pastime he took up cameo-cutting—re-creating for himself both the tools and the technique necessary for the pursuit of this delicate and trying art. For a while he had a mild success at cutting portrait cameos, but the eye strain involved in such fine work forced him to give up the art, whereupon he turned to sculpture in a larger form. His first sculptural works were reliefs in the manner of Thorvaldsen. These, in fine, amounted to greatly enlarged cameos. From bas-reliefs he progressed to making life-sized portrait busts and figures in the round. The *Indian Girl* is reputed to be his first attempt at a full-length figure—it is certainly no mean achievement, coming as it did, from the hand of an up-state carpenter in 1856. Its success led him to try another full-length figure, this time a nude, *The White Captive,* which seemed to be quite a daring

and unconventional performance. A visitor to his studio, Anson G. Chester, describing the works displayed there says of this figure:

But, above all, was a model, a simulacrum, of "The White Captive"—intended as a companion to Palmer's glorious statue of the "Indian Girl"—a life-size female figure, entirely nude. The right arm of the statue is bound, by the wrist, to a tree; the left arm is placed behind the back. This is a bold step in advance of custom and conventionalism, but it is one which we can but approve. In most female figures wrought by the sculptor's chisel there is some attitude or appliance indicative of conscious shame. In this there is nothing of the sort. And why should there be? Eve's modesty was her original inheritance. When she was pure she knew not she was naked. It was guilt that set her to sewing fig-leaves. . . . We cordially commend Palmer for his independence in this direction. If the world is not extra squeamish, this one manly innovation will be the making of him. . . . Palmer's star is in the ascendant. It still swims the liquid ether—it is not yet moored in the zenith. We are to hear of great achievements before it leaves off climbing. Let us wait and watch.[37]

The White Captive enjoyed, in its way, the same sort of success that had attended the showing of Powers' *Greek Slave,* and for the same reasons, and with the same kind of defense by the clergy. It is, however, quite unlike the *Greek Slave,* much less dependent on classical prototypes and much more of a demonstration of sure anatomical knowledge than the *Slave* or any other work that the Sublime Mechanic Powers was ever able to make. In spite of the praise of press and pulpit, Jarves claimed it was impossible for him to think of anything but meat while looking at *The White Captive*—it was perhaps a little too realistic.

Lorado Taft, in his *History of American Sculpture,* reaches his account of Palmer with an almost audible sigh of relief. After carefully refraining from saying, through many pages, that American sculpture before Palmer seemed scarcely worth recording, he grew quite lyrical over Palmer's works, and with reason.

The studio of Erastus Palmer must have been a singularly exotic ornament in the town of Albany, and visitors to the studio all said it was indeed a bit of Rome transplanted to the banks of the Hudson. In the decade 1840–1850 Albany was a busy commercial depot and transportation center through which, in season, flowed tourists bound for the Great Falls of Niagara and a con-

[37] *Cosmopolitan Art Journal,* II (1858).

tinuous stream of emigrants heading further west to settle. Somewhat aloof from the turmoil there existed a staid society composed of the rather baronial remnants of old Dutch landowning families. In this smoke and hurry of travel and the ponderous pleasures of the gelid social atmosphere, Palmer's art came into flower.

Palmer's studio, which gave Henry Tuckerman such a twinge of "homesickness" for Rome, was organized and run with a thoroughly American efficiency. Everything was very businesslike and orderly; each work progressed through the rooms of the studio, advancing through the various stages to completion almost as though the marble blocks were on an assembly line. In spite of this American touch, the work of the studio was done by a crew of workmen in the Italian fashion. Among these workmen were several young American apprentices learning the art. Launt Thompson and Charles Calverly, both well-known New York sculptors of a later day, were trained here under the eye of the Albany master.

By 1856 Palmer's works had received so much favorable notice that a body of eminent clergymen, whose potence as art critics had already been proven by Powers, invited Palmer to show his work in New York City at the hall belonging to the Church of the Divine Unity on Broadway. The exhibition here of the "Palmer Marbles" brought nation-wide attention to this wonderful sculptor who had learned his art unaided in up-state New York, disdaining to taint his native genius among the ruins and academies of the Art-Lands of Europe. When news of the exhibition traveled to Boston, a group of the most eminent citizens of the New England metropolis took the liberty of expressing their strong desire that Mr. Palmer would find it convenient to exhibit the same for a while in Boston. The group included such noted personalities as Edward Everett, Longfellow, Quincy, Prescott, Jared Sparks, Lowell, and Louis Agassiz.

It is interesting to note how quickly the sculptors took advantage of the early daguerreotypes and photographs as a means of popularizing their works. Palmer was one of the first of these, and photographs of his religious reliefs were sold by the hundreds to appear in provincial parlors throughout the state. Today one still finds these photographs shrined deep in heavily molded walnut "bull's eye" frames hung over the parlor mantel in country hotels. Occasionally, in the larger establishments are

to be seen the replicas in white marble or "Parian" looking as though made of dusty artificial snow.

A German art critic was enabled to publish an article on Palmer's work in 1865 based entirely on the study of photographs imported from America—and the romance of the art historian and his gray world of photographs was on its way to becoming a national vice. When Powers was shown a daguerreotype of one of Palmer's works he was astonished to find that the artist had never been abroad to study. "He never needs to come," said Hiram, glad, perhaps, that such a formidable rival showed little interest in leaving Albany and relieved that his own position as the leading Yankee genius in Italy would not be endangered.

The strong religious turn in Palmer's character caused him to execute many works inspired by religious subjects, and one is led to believe, in view of the excellence of his work, that through his religious experience and his craftsman's training Palmer approached more closely than many of the other American sculptors to the mystery which gave greatness to the art of the ancients. His remark that the function of art was to represent by effects rather than to imitate by copying must have sounded like a blasphemous heresy to the followers of Canova who had spent their lives feebly repeating the classic errors of the Italian master.

Jarves says of Palmer: [He] typifies in himself American art in bondage. The will and feeling to be original and inventive are there, but they are in the bonds of materialism and inexperience."[38]

William Wetmore Story: The Boston Lawyer in Rome

FOR William Story life held out every promise of happiness and fulfillment. To his contemporaries he seemed richly endowed almost beyond belief. He was brilliant, witty, versatile, wealthy, of good family; a successful lawyer, author, poet, and—as some believed—a sculptor. Added to all this was his impeccable Boston Brahmin background. He was born in Salem in 1819 and at the age of ten was taken to live in Cambridge, where his father, then an Associate Justice of the United States Supreme Court, was a founder of and teacher in the Harvard Law School.

Among the intimate friends of William Story's child-

[38] Jarves, Art Idea (1864).

hood and youth were James Russell Lowell, Charles Sumner, Thomas Wentworth Higginson, and many others who were later to become nationally known figures. In 1838 Story graduated from Harvard, and on his graduation from the Law School in 1840 he entered the Boston law firm of Hillard and Sumner. During his youth he had developed an interest in poetry, painting, sculpture, and music. When his father died in 1845 he was elected by the trustees of Mount Auburn Cemetery, solely on the strength of his kinship and his amateur interest in sculpture, to execute a life-size portrait statue of Judge Story, to be placed in the memorial chapel at the cemetery.

To prepare himself to carry out this commission he went to Italy in 1847 and from that time forth became more and more eager to give up the law entirely in favor of sculpture, in spite of strong opposition from his family and friends—not to mention some very weighty misgivings on the part of his own New England conscience. But from the moment he put foot on Italian soil he was a willing captive to its spell, and a career as a sculptor seemed to offer legitimate reasons for not returning to Boston and the law. In 1856 he settled permanently in Rome, where he soon became one of the leading figures in the foreign colony. When his fame was at its height, in 1877, he made a triumphal tour of the United States. On his return to Italy he was considered the outstanding American exponent of the arts. He died at his daughter's summer villa at Vallombrosa in 1895.

Among his contemporaries only Nathaniel Hawthorne, a fellow townsman from Story's native Salem, seems to have penetrated beneath the dashing pose and elegant social mask in which the artist-poet appeared to his numerous admirers. Hawthorne's keen perception detected, under the glittering panoply of success and promise, the mark of bitter discontent and unhappiness. He says: "Mr. Story is the most variously accomplished and brilliant person, the fullest of social life and fire, whom I ever met; . . . he kept us amused and entertained the whole day long. . . Still, though he bubbled and brimmed over with fun, he left the impression on me that . . . there is a pain and care, bred, it may be, out of the very richness of his gifts and abundance of his outward prosperity."

Curiously enough, almost every other mention of Story in Hawthorne's *Note Books* is in connection with some morbid or violent fantasy related by Story. At one meeting they talk of the evil eye; at another, Story dilates on the unluckiness of Friday; again, he proposes a fable on the Bluebeard theme. On a carriage drive through Rome he explains in detail some peculiarly horrible Italian burial customs. Later he tells a tale of a dead body reduced by some mysterious process to a small stone set in a ring which poisons the life of the wearer—an idea for a story worthy of Hawthorne himself and one he admits he wished he had thought of first.

William Story's mother thought him an utter fool—and said as much—for abandoning an assuredly successful career as a Boston lawyer for the questionable pursuit of an art he was never able to master. Story's tragedy, which doubtless gave him the air of unhappiness that Hawthorne sensed, was the realization that he could never achieve his romantic ideal of being a great sculptor, though he could, and did, act the part to perfection. His tragedy was the tragedy of too easy success, too many kinds of success. Though many people believed him to be a genius and though he lived in a Roman *palazzo* for over forty years surrounded with all the necessary scenery and props appropriate to the role of a great artist, the man knew himself to be a gilded amateur. He was too intelligent not to realize that it takes more than praise and versatility to make a sculptor and he knew that there was no substitute for his lack of early training.

This "pain and care," this underlying unhappiness, was the product of inner tensions and pressures. Under a surfeit of charming circumstances his spirit was chafed by the snaffle of frustration and indecision. This may account for his interest in the morbid and theatrical and for his splurging activities in all directions.

Story found himself, as it were, suspended in a delectable Italian dream world, vacillating amid half careers, a victim of the meager, cold Art-Life, or what passed for Art-Life in New England during his formative years. The scholastic atmosphere of Cambridge had burdened him with such a literary turn of mind that, even as a boy, he called the old swimming hole up the Charles River "the Bowre of Blisse" after Spenser. And so one discovers him well along in life, holding in his hands the fragments of three of four careers. Only one of these came anywhere near completion—the career he enjoyed most, naturally, the career that was the most perfect escape from reality— the career of being a Roman. From his love of all things

Roman grew his book *Roba di Roma,* a collection of essays on the endlessly multiplied curios and treasures of old Rome. His other careers were all unfinished, unresolved to any satisfying completion. That of lawyer, the career for which he was best fitted by tradition and training, he gave up at its beginning. That of sculptor, for which, possibly, he was best suited temperamentally, he started with no preparation except a romantic desire that served but weakly in place of strong plastic perceptions and long labor. As poet and essayist he followed in the footsteps of others.

But time has a way of covering such wounds; gradually, as his popular successes multiplied, the outward man became more real than the inner. As his contemporaries read significance into the cold attitudes of his sculptural works so did they find satisfaction in the pose of the actor-artist who appeared to them in velvet beret and Norfolk jacket surrounded by all sorts of romantic associations.

Yet in spite of Story's wide popular esteem, Henry James, writing only a few years after Story's death, says: "His imaginåtion, of necessity, went in preference to the figure for which accessories were of the essence; which is doubtless a proof . . . that he was not with that last intensity a sculptor. Had he been this he would not, in all probability, have been also with such intensity . . . so many other things; a man of ideas—of *other* ideas, of other curiosities. . . And we see that, if the approach to final form be through concentration, he was not concentrated. If sculpture be a thing of supreme intimacy he was not supremely intimate. He had, in a word, too many friends for any one of them to have succeeded in establishing absolute rights."

Story's imagination was, indeed, almost entirely literary, two dimensional, and literal. His knowledge of anatomy was sufficient to enable him to write a book on the subject, but his plastic grasp of the sculptural problems involved was so feeble that he scarcely ever attempted a full-length standing figure, and he avoided the nude as unsuited to the moral and sculptural needs of his time. Apparently very few of his effigies had sufficient vitality to stand upright—they recline, heavily draped against their self-generated cold, in elegant chairs of classic design. All of them are well bolstered with poetic libretti and all sorts of legally provable facts and accessories before and after the facts, to explain their imprisonment in

stone. A strain of operatic tragedy threads throughout his written works in poem, essay, and drama and in the violent scenes he tried so valiantly to portray in marble. As a sculptor his concerns were the concerns of a lawyer and his works constitute a sort of morbid chamber of horrors where all the criminals and madmen of history and legend pay the price of eternal immobility. Here is Cleopatra, the victim of violent passions, contemplating suicide; there is Medea, the unnatural mother, preparing to murder her children; Salome awaits the beheading of her beloved; there is Saul in his madness; old Lear; and, last but not least, Little Red Riding Hood and the Wolf, a subject chosen with incongruous felicity.

Today his writings, with, ironically enough, the possible exception of his legal works, are of value and interest only to the historian of manners who, like Henry James, seeks to evoke the ghosts of a forgotten and vanished society. Unquestionably his best works were the monumental biography of his father and the legal treatises compiled before he went to Rome. Interest in him is limited now almost exclusively to literary historians tracking down hints and traces of Thackeray or Walter Savage Landor. Perhaps he is best known for his long intimate friendship with Robert and Elizabeth Barrett Browning, the companions and literary models of his early Italian days.

For many years the Storys' apartment in the Palazzo Barberini was a gathering place for all the noted visitors staying in Rome. The roster of their guests is an almost complete list of all the notables who traveled in Italy in the mid-nineteenth century. Besides the literary figures already mentioned, there were dignitaries of the Roman Church, Roman princes, musicians, actors, statesmen, and Bostonians. By one of those marvelously odd tricks of fate which bring about the most unimaginable occurrences, William Story's daughter Edith married the Marchese Simone Peruzzi de' Medici, a descendant of the ancient ennobled family of bankers and legal heir to the exalted name of Medici. Thus was the granddaughter of an American Supreme Court Justice transformed into a Medici, a figure in Italian court circles, where her husband was chamberlain to King Victor Emmanuel II and King Humbert.

Story's fame as a sculptor was chiefly due to Pope Pius IX, who generously paid the expenses of shipping his Cleopatra and his Libyan Sibyl to the London Exposition in 1862, where they became the sensation of the Roman sculpture display and the especial favorites of Victorian critics. But Story was also indebted to Hawthorne, who, in his novel *The Marble Faun* describes at length the *Cleopatra,* which thereby gained a tremendous notoriety among novel readers and a literary fame that was, all things considered, quite in keeping.

In his *Note-Books* Hawthorne says of the *Cleopatra:* "We have seen . . . William Story's *Cleopatra*—a work of genuine thought and energy, representing a terribly dangerous woman; quiet enough for the moment, but very likely to spring upon you like a tigress." Story's poem "Cleopatra"—too long to be given here entire— furnishes whatever vitality and fire the sculpture seems so notably to lack today. Considering its Victorian date the poem shows an astonishing passion and sensuality. The poem is in reality the script of a drama without which the statue is a limp marionette—the tigerishness is now perceptible only in the words of the poem.

Henry James, unwilling to commit himself, speaks of the poem and the statue with admirable restraint: "It was impossible to be more interested in the things of the mind and in the forms and combinations into which they over-flow. The question of expression and style haunted him; the question of representation by words was ever as present to him as that of representation by marble or by bronze. Once in a while these ideas move him in the same direction with equal force; he produced, for in-stance, two Cleopatras, and it is difficult to say that the versified, the best of his shorter poems, is not as 'good' as the so interesting statue with which it competes."

The versified Cleopatra reads in part:

> Here, Charmian, take my bracelets,
> They bar with purple stain
> My arms; turn over my pillows—
> They are hot where I have lain:
> Open the lattice wider,
> A gauze o'er my bosom throw,
> And let me inhale the odours
> That over the garden blow.
>
> . . . .
>
> I will lie and dream of the past time,
> Aeons of thought away,
> And through the jungle of memory
> Loosen my fancy to play;
> When, a smooth and velvety tiger,
> Ribbed with yellow and black,
> Supple and cushion-footed,
> I wandered, where never the track

> Of a human creature had rustled
> The silence of mighty woods,
> And, fierce in a tyrannous freedom,
> I knew but the law of my moods.
> The elephant, trumpeting, started,
> When he heard my footsteps near,
> And the spotted giraffes fled wildly
> In a yellow cloud of fear.
> I sucked in the noontide splendour,
> Quivering along the glade,
> Or yawning, panting, and dreaming,
> Basked in the tamarisk shade,
> Till I heard my wild mate roaring,
> As the shadows of night came on
> To brood in the trees' thick branches,
> And the shadow of sleep was gone;
> Then I roused and roared in answer,
> And unsheathed from my cushioned feet
> My curving claws, and stretched me
> And wandered my mate to greet.
> We toyed in the amber moonlight,
> Upon the warm flat sand,
> And struck at each other our massive arms—
> How powerful he was and grand!
> His yellow eyes flashed fiercely
> As he crouched and gazed at me,
> And his quivering tail, like a serpent,
> Twitched, curving nervously.
> Then like a storm he seized me,
> With a wild triumphant cry,
> And we met, as two clouds in heaven
> When thunders before them fly.
> We grappled and struggled together,
> For his love like his rage was rude;
> And his teeth in the swelling folds of my neck
> At times, in our play, drew blood.
> Often another suitor—
> For I was flexile and fair—
> Fought for me in the moonlight,
> While I lay crouching there,
> Till his blood was drained by the desert;
> And, ruffled with triumph and power,
> He licked me and lay beside me
> To breathe him a vast half-hour.
>
> . . . .
>
> Come to my arms, my hero,
> The shadows of twilight grow,
> And the tiger's ancient fierceness
> In my veins begins to flow.
> Come not with cringing to sue me!
> Take me with triumph and power,
> As a warrior storms a fortress!
> I will not shrink or cower.

Come, as you came in the desert,
Ere we were women and men,
When the tiger passions were in us,
And love as you loved me then!

His fame was, however, short-lived, and as early as 1873 we find one outspoken visitor to his studio remarking, "We went to Mr. Story's studio, and oh! how he does spoil nice blocks of white marble. Nothing but Sibyls on all sides, sitting, standing, legs crossed, legs uncrossed, and all with the same expression as if they smelt something wrong. Call him a genius! I don't see it."[39] The judgment is unkind perhaps but in any case it set the keynote for the judgment of future generations.

Though his friends and admirers always classed Story far above the mechanic sculptors of his time, he nevertheless fell under the spell of the machine—in his own literary way. In his book on anatomy and proportion in sculpture he proposes reliance on mathematical formulas and measurements—in other words a mechanical system for success in sculpture. Thus did the machine dominate his work, though it was made acceptable to him by being disguised as a literary idea with pleasing classical associations.

William Rimmer: Artist, Physician, Eccentric

If the tragedy of William Story was the early realization that true artistic fulfillment would always be beyond his untrained grasp because of his own limitations, the tragedy of William Rimmer lay in another direction, and much farther down in the depths of despair. Rimmer knew that he had great possibilities—skill, imagination, vision, power—but circumstances beyond his control always contrived to defeat him before he had half a chance to show what he could do. Whereas Story, all his life, was surrounded with every advantage and comfort, the center of a brilliant and congenial social circle wherever he went, William Rimmer struggled alone in friendlessness and neglect in the stony, self-centered cultural deserts of suburban Boston. While the press lavished praise upon every bungler who could afford the price of a block of marble in which to perpetrate sentimental inanities, Rimmer remained unknown. The names of Michael Angelo and Phidias were indiscriminately linked with those of Powers, Mozier, Crawford, Ives,

while Rimmer—the only man of the group even faintly worthy of such a compliment—was vainly trying to support his family as a physician in the little settlements of quarrymen near the granite pits of Quincy, Massachusetts.

Earlier Rimmer had worked in Brockton as a cobbler. It is to be regretted that Hawthorne never discovered Rimmer nor heard the strange story of his life, for a more perfect Hawthorne character and plot could scarcely be imagined. Spiritually William Rimmer was prematurely aged by being burdened as a youth with the bitter confidences of his father, Thomas—a strange, violent character about whom hung mysterious and unsubstantiated legends of his royal ancestry similar to those which shroud the ancestry of Audubon. William Rimmer was prematurely aged physically by overwork and the sharp blows of fate—the successive deaths of his sons, poverty, and lack of appreciation. William inherited from his father, along with the royal legend, a thorniness of character, an excessive shyness, and an obtuse pride which made it difficult for him to make and keep sympathetic contacts with other people.

A wonderful and tragic personal symbolism pervades his work in sculpture and in drawing. In the drawings there is the vast evening sadness of space over boundless plains; the horizon lies at terrible distances, unattainable and remote; his figures float in the air, swooning, falling, dying. Chained monsters, exquisitely constructed, writhe in agony; winged genii falter in their flight; marvelous horses plunge and rear in nervous excitement. Rare indeed were the American artists of his time who could draw with such freedom and understanding.

In Rimmer's sculpture the history of his pain and defeat at the hands of a mercenary age is told in granite, bronze, and a few bits of chipped plaster. For years these works lay forgotten in the dust of art-school attics, or interred in the mortuary caverns of museum basements while museum galleries became cluttered with expensive European kickshaws and parlor trophies.

As New England had allowed Allston to wither away from neglect, while its imagination was chained to the written words of polite authors and the close-figured ledgers of State Street, so, again, did she allow another and greater artist to perish spiritually in her well-stayed literary bosom. Fat commissions for public monuments were handed out to feeble, facile socialite amateurs or to

[39] Mrs. Henry Adams, *The Letters of Mrs. Henry Adams, 1865–1883;* ed. by Ward Thoron (Boston, 1936).

artists with trumped-up European reputations while Rimmer's talents were wasted for lack of opportunity.

Rimmer's earliest existing sculptural work, the product of his youth, is a statuette called *Despair;* it is not the familiar tombstone figure of a weeping angel that his contemporaries would have made; this is not the despair of genteel women—this is the despair, dry-eyed, tense, explosive, of a young man who had been given every opportunity to become intimately acquainted with the subject through personal experience. It was not something he had read about, its shape and shadow had often been described to him by his father. Beneath the small plaster hand of this statuette, clapped over its anguished mouth, lies perhaps the secret that Thomas Rimmer and his family so successfully suppressed.

Rimmer's head of Saint Stephen, carved in Quincy granite, was one of the few pieces of sculpture of that day (1860) to be carved direct in native stone. It was wrenched from the rock by main force, in the brief space of one month. There were no soft stages through clay and plaster models, no docile Italian stonecutters did the laborious work, no picturesque model posed except in the mind of the artist, who wept with physical and nervous exhaustion as he made it.

The *Falling Gladiator,* an attempt to represent in sculpture a most difficult involuntary action, was a marvel of anatomical knowledge. It was a tour de force of which no other American sculptor was then capable. It was of such extraordinary faithfulness, so plastic, that when it was exhibited in the Paris Salon of 1863 some people said it was made by trickery. They claimed, in their smug ignorance, that it had been cast from a living model—an obviously impossible feat. Thus by the vagaries of academicians was Rimmer robbed of possible artistic fame during his lifetime. Ironically enough, the same sort of claim by a salon jury fifteen years later and the scandal created at that time over the *Age of Bronze* by Rodin made the French sculptor famous. In Rimmer's *Falling Gladiator* is symbolized the death of the neoclassic style and subject, and in it one sees foreshadowed the beginnings of plastic and impressionistic realism that was to be so much admired in the works of later sculptors.

The *Fighting Lions,* perhaps the best piece of animal sculpture produced in America in the nineteenth century, makes even the beasts of Barye seem like tame desk ornaments, paperweights. These animals of Rimmer's are not mechanical forms reproduced from nature—photographed by mere skill of hand and eye. Rimmer absorbed the spirit of leonine ferocity by close study of the animal before beginning to work, in the same way that the great Chinese painters prepared themselves to create the spirit rather than the shell of reality. In general the American sculptors of the day had little feeling for animals—one need only compare Rimmer's lions with the awkward, ludicrous animals designed by Crawford to see the infinite superiority of Rimmer's knowledge. However, the connoisseurs of the time would have none of his works, it is only by accident and the efforts of a few sculptors that any of the works of Rimmer have been cast in bronze —preserved for new neglect.

What more perfect symbol could be found for the career of William Rimmer than his own bronze *The Dying Centaur?* A wild pagan creature, half man, half myth, sinking to the earth, with amputated arm stretching its handless stump to a pitiless Puritan sky. This was what society could do to an artist who loved art more than literature, who dared to express ideas by form rather than by the trumpery props prescribed by convention. They could let him squander his great talents and exhaust his mind lecturing on anatomy before a blackboard on whose surface he cast a thousand masterly sketches with a prodigal hand for the edification of a class of young ladies. However, the admiration and gratitude of his young pupils must have been balm though it came late to the wound.

Rimmer's acquaintance as a doctor with the miseries of his poor patients at the granite quarry and in the factories of Brockton gave him a far deeper understanding of humanity than any of the other sculptors enjoyed. His expert knowledge of human anatomy allowed his artistic imagination to break free from the shackles of current convention in his sculpture and in his drawings. Rimmer was, in large part, his own patron—a sufficiently tragic dilemma for any artist. There was scarcely anyone in America who could understand him. Hawthorne might have, Melville might have, a few artists did, but the people who gave out commissions and prizes for the most part preferred safe, scholarly sentiment to anything that smacked of social thought. What Rimmer's notebooks and diaries might reveal we can only guess at from the carefully censored bits that have been published. One would like to know more about this man.

The only happy time of his life was the four-year period spent as director of the School of Design for Women at Cooper Union. Old Peter Cooper must have understood Rimmer's interest in the workingman, but apparently Rimmer had by then become too embittered and eccentric for even the liberal officers of the Cooper Union to endure.

The works of William Rimmer, though two of them bear classical titles (*The Falling Gladiator* and *The Dying Centaur*), are unique among the products of American sculptors of his time in that they lean on no literary or biographical buttresses. They are presented in the modern way, unadorned with anecdote, as direct studies in the art of sculpture, not as petrified dramas.

However far ahead of his contemporaries Rimmer was as a creative artist, one final act in his career reveals him as a man of his time. Even he, at last, succumbed to the blandishments of the machine and the "statuary business." Sometime about 1875 he became interested in the promotion of a stock company—the American Photo Sculpture Company—for which he wrote an enthusiastic prospectus. The backers of the company wished to use his name to add the necessary note of artistic integrity to a tawdry business scheme. They expected to reap large profits from the mechanical mass production of portrait busts. The project, however, was a failure. Rimmer's friends considered it an unaccountable idiosyncracy that so great an artist should have been taken in by such a crass scheme. Possibly it was, on his part, a last gesture of defiance, as though in spite, against a society which had spurned his best efforts. Rimmer was no business man or he certainly would have realized that the photograph had ruined that once "lucrative business," the making of portrait busts.

Horatio Greenough: The Honest Yankee Stonecutter

WITHOUT any question Horatio Greenough—the *first* American sculptor of the First American School of Sculpture—is by far the most important man in the group. It is true that as a sculptor he was time-bound like his contemporaries and his works in marble are not of the first importance *as sculpture*. However, unlike his fellow sculptors Greenough learned from his craft as a hewer of stone some of the deeper truths of art and life. His marbles were whetstones upon which he sharpened the blade of his intellect. His sculpture would seem to be a by-product of his search for truth. In learning to know his tools and materials and the processes of sculpture, the mind of the artist was molded by his art. In the development of his ideas he penetrated to the bedrock where the primal crystals of wisdom lie.

No one could remark of Greenough, as Jarves says of the other sculptors of his school, that he was "speedily seduced into the facile path of realism by the national bias to the material and practical."[40] No other American sculptor of his time had the candor and modesty to admit in print at the outset of his career: "I fear that the circumstances under which I began my career will ever prevent me realizing my idea of what sculpture should be . . . I cannot pretend to occupy any space in a work consecrated to American art. . . . I began to *study* art in Rome, in 1826. Until then I had rather amused myself with clay and marble. When I say that those materials were familiar to my touch, I say all that I profited by my boyish efforts. They were rude. I lived with poets and poetry, and could not then see that my art was to be studied from folk who ate their three meals every day. . . . It was not until I had run through all the galleries and studio of Rome, and had had under my eye the genial forms of Italy that I began to feel nature's value. I had before adored her, but as a Persian does the sun, with my face to the earth. I then began to examine her—and entered on that course of study in which I am still toiling."[41]

Though the works of almost every other American sculptor of his time enjoyed unstinted praise from credulous admirers, the works of Greenough, pioneering in an exotic field, were but indifferently received when first shown in America. They had, of course, a certain amount of curiosity value, being, it was supposed, the first works in sculpture to be made by an American. Greenough's first ideal work, the *Chanting Cherubs,* when exhibited at the Boston Athenaeum filled Allston with pleasure and pride; other Bostonians thought the naked cherubs shockingly immoral. When they were exhibited in New York no one seemed particularly shocked but most of the visitors to the exhibition felt that they had been humbugged. A friend of the sculptor wrote, "The Cherubs failed here, owing it is said to their name. Our literal folk actually supposed that they were to sing, and when

[40] J. J. Jarves, *The Art Idea* (1864).
[41] William Dunlap, *History of the Rise and Progress of the Arts of Design in the United States* (1834).

the man turned them round in order to exhibit them in a different position they exclaimed, 'Ah, he is going to wind them up: we shall hear them now'." The New Yorkers felt swindled out of an amusing show. Our reporter continues, "I wish the scene of this story lay anywhere but in New York, but it cannot be helped, and I must continue to consider my townsmen as a race of cheating, lying, money-getting blockheads."[42]

If however the critics and connoisseurs at home did not appreciate Greenough's work, a few of the leading men of the time saw in the young Greenough a man of unusual promise. The critical mind of Fenimore Cooper was immediately attracted by him; from their first meeting in Florence in 1829 they were fast friends. Greenough writes, "Fenimore Cooper saved me from despair. . . . He employed me as I wished to be employed; with a commission for original work and has, up to this moment, been a father to me in kindness."[43]

But the painter Washington Allston was the most important influence the sculptor knew during his formative years. In 1833 Greenough writes, "Allston was to me a father, in what concerned my progress of every kind. He taught me first how to discriminate, how to think, how to feel. Before I knew him I felt strongly but blindly . . . if I should never pass mediocrity, I should attribute it to my absence from him. So adapted did he seem to kindle and enlighten me, making me no longer myself, but, as it were, an emanation of his own soul."[44] It was Allston who brought Greenough to the attention of Daniel Webster when Congress was planning to order a statue of Washington for the Capitol.

According to Jarves, "We were as fortunate in having Horatio Greenough for a pioneer in this direction as Allston in the sister-art. Both were true artists, in advance of their times, inspired by the best examples of the old schools, though in execution unequal to their conceptions . . . his [Greenough's] whole career was an example in the right direction . . In his Washington he rises above mere portraiture, and seeks to symbolize, in a colossal statue of god-like form, the nation's cherished 'father.' As we rise to the level of his sympathies and knowledge, so shall we better understand him and appreciate his efforts."[45]

Cooper, warning Greenough of the kind of reception to expect for his Washington in America, writes (1836): "As respects your statue, talk not, touch not, think not. You are in a country in which every man swaggers and talks, knowledge or no knowledge; brains or no brains; taste or no taste. They are all *ex nato* connoisseurs, politicians, religionists, and every man's equal, and all men's betters. In short you are to expect your own matured and classical thoughts will be estimated by the same rules as they estimate pork, and rum, and cotton. Luckily you get a pretty good sum, and the statue that has cost *them* $20,000 may stand some chance. Alas! my good Greenough, this is no region of poets, so sell your wares and shut your ears."[46]

Perhaps the Washington is not the greatest piece of sculpture made in the nineteenth century, but it is an important document of American art history, its subject is of prime significance, and the artist is in every way deserving of admiration and respect. The statue of Washington has always been unlucky. When it was first placed in the rotunda of the Capitol, where it was purposely designed to stand, its weight was judged too great for the floor of the building to support. The nude torso was of course found shocking, Washington could be symbolized apparently by a suit of clothes but to suggest, as Greenough did, that he was man, was outrageous.[47] The homegrown connoisseurs who passed it mocked its dignified gestures and claimed that the sculptor had petrified Washington in the act of saying "Here is my sword—my clothes are in the Patent Office, yonder." At great cost the statue was moved out-of-doors and set up in the Capitol grounds, surrounded with inappropriate flowerbeds and lamp-posts and railings that obstructed the best views of the sculpture. Here it suffered the rigors of the weather and the indignities of birds unprotected until it was moved, in 1908, to the "Smithsonian Palace," a building whose dark "mediaeval confusions" caused Greenough to shudder uneasily when he first saw it. Surely Greenough's Washington, after a century of shameful treat-

---

[42] J. F. Cooper, *Correspondence* (1832).
[43] Dunlap, *op. cit.*
[44] *Ibid.*
[45] Jarves, *The Art Idea.*

[46] Cooper, *Correspondence* (1836).
[47] Davy Crockett, an *ex nato* connoisseur from the Tennessee canebrakes, remarked after seeing Chantrey's statue of Washington at Boston in 1834, "I do not like the statue of Washington in the State-House. They have a Roman gown on him, and he was an American; this ain't right. They did the better thing at Richmond, in Virginia, where they have him in the old blue and buff. He belonged to his country—heart, soul, and body and I dont want any other [country] to have any part of him—not even his clothes."—*The Life of David Crockett . . . With His Triumphal Tour through the Northern States.* New York, n.d.

ment, deserves a better fate. Such an obviously important example of the American neoclassic school of sculpture would certainly be at home in the new National Gallery —a building only faintly less Roman in style than the sculpture.

In his time Greenough was misunderstood and misprized—he was briefly valued by some as a sculptor; a few, Emerson among them, recognized the importance of his ideas. Today he is forgotten. Though the modern art world flourishes on theories of functionalism which he first pointed out, these theories are credited to twentieth-century architects and imported industrial designers. It is true Greenough did not live to develop his ideas, he left no followers. The way he pointed out, the moral virtue of honest craftsmanship unadorned with applied and borrowed embellishments, was completely ignored. No one followed in his footsteps, and a rank growth of weeds and briers made the path uninviting. It was too hard a road, uphill all the way, too precipitous to attract the success-bound journeyman. Fine art and the making of things were believed to be poles apart, between stood the Hydra of Fashion which Greenough called "the instinctive effort of the stationary to pass itself off for progress."

After reading his few essays and fragmentary writings on art one begins to feel that in justice Greenough should be classed with that small select company of original minds which America produced in the early nineteenth century. If he had been given a few more years to pursue his theory to its ultimate conclusions, he would surely stand with the other leading American thinkers of the time, with Emerson, Theodore Parker, Thoreau, and Dr. Holmes. Because the Fates dealt peremptorily with him, cutting him off in his prime, because his writings are few, and his ideas not fully developed, are they any the less significant? Are his broad vision and intellectual integrity reduced to trifling because his contemporaries pushed him into oblivion in their blind rush into the horrors of 'civil war and on into the tawdry corruption of the "Great Barbecue" that followed in the gilded age?

America produced only one sculptor in the early nineteenth century who had the courage and ability to draw important philosophical conclusions from his craft, only Greenough had the moral stamina to stick to his unpopular convictions in the face of accepted tradition, convention, taboo, and Academy, Royal or otherwise. We cannot afford to ignore any man of whom Emerson said, "Horatio Greenough, lately returned from Italy, came here and spent the day,—an extraordinary man, a man of sense, of virtue, and rare elevation of thought and carriage. One thought of heroes—of Alfieri, of Michaelangelo, of Leonardo da Vinci. How old? 'Forty-seven years of joy have I lived' was his answer. He makes most of my accustomed stars pale by his clear light. His magnanimity, his idea of a great man, his courage, and cheer, and self-reliance, and depth, and self-derived knowledge, charmed and invigorated me as none has . . . these many months . . . The grandest of democrats. His democracy is very deep, and for the most part free from crochets,—not quite,— and philosophical."[48]

As William Rimmer stands far above his contemporaries as a sculptor, Greenough towers above them as a man, as a thinker. Perhaps it will be said that the conception of one major idea does not make a man into a great philosopher—perhaps not. But consider Greenough's background and training; observe the other artists of his time and their superficial ideas; contrast the far-reaching significance of his conception of functionalism and organic relationships as the basis of beauty with their shallow mouthings of mechanical and literary formulas. Greenough's theory, even though only partially developed, placed the entity we call "art" directly in its normal relation to life.

His study of anatomy did not lead him off into a scholarly pedantic dead end in classical literature as it did William Story. It led Greenough to a thoughtful consideration of comparative anatomy, and from this study he deduced that the infinite variations of anatomical structure are the controlled, purposeful design suiting organization to use—or, as we would say today, form follows function. As this idea began to exfoliate he began to pierce further into a philosophical understanding of the importance of this basic idea in its application to other things than anatomy. He judged by his new standard not only works of art as functional organizations but also architecture—quickly demolishing the pretensions of the so-called "Greek Revival." From architecture he passed on to the beginnings of a criticism of the social structure and aesthetic theories. Burke's pronunciamentos on the beautiful wither to paltry sophistry before Greenough's theory.

[48] R. W. Emerson, *Journals* (1852).

He was more truly Greek than any of the mechano-Phidian geniuses in sculpture. They copied shapes while he comprehended principles. He approached the basic causes and principles of Aristotle and in this grasped at the fringes of a vast world of Oriental wisdom that had been forgotten in European art for centuries. Greenough's "Stonecutter's Creed" contains in three simple sentences the seed of his best thought:

> By beauty I mean the promise of function.
> By action I mean the presence of function.
> By character I mean the record of function.

There is in his little book of essays a transcendental point where suddenly he is no longer criticizing the incongruous curiosities of art in America in 1851. Suddenly he speaks as though he had attained an inner enlightenment, a clarification and unity of spirit through the contemplation of his theory and the results of his prime idea. There is a Himalayan air of simplicity and wisdom in his conclusions that is worthy of an Asiatic sage.

His essay on "Relative and Independent Beauty" is permeated with an extraordinary Oriental tone:

> There are threads of relation which lead me from my specialty to the specialties of other men . . . I lay my artistic dogma at the feet of science; I test it by the traditional lore of handicraft; I seek a confirmation of these my inductions, or a contradiction and refutation of them . . . I let them lead me as a child.

· · · · ·

I understand by embellishment, THE INSTINCTIVE EFFORT OF INFANT CIVILIZATION TO DISGUISE ITS INCOMPLETENESS, EVEN AS GOD'S COMPLETENESS IS TO INFANT SCIENCE DISGUISED. . . . I base my opinion of embellishment upon the hypothesis that there is not one truth in religion, another in mathematics, and a third in physics and in art; but that there is one truth, even as one God, and that organization is his utterance. . . .The normal development of beauty is through action to completeness. The invariable development of embellishment and decoration is more embellishment and more decoration. . . . but where is the first downward step? I maintain that the first downward step was *the introduction of the first inorganic, non-functional element, whether of shape or color.* If I be told that such a system as mine would produce *nakedness,* I accept the omen. In nakedness I behold the majesty of the essential, instead of the trappings of pretension. . . . The aim of the artist, therefore should be first to seek the essential; when the essential hath been found, then, if ever, will be time to commence embellishment . . . the essential, when found, will be complete. . . . In a

word, completeness is the absolute utterance of the Godhead . . . the completeness of the sea . . . the completeness of the earth, whose every atom is a microcosm; the completeness of the human body, where all relations are resumed at once and dominated . . . I hold the human body, therefore, to be a multiform command. Its capacities are the law and gauge of manhood as connected with earth. I hold the blessings attendant upon obedience to this command, to be the yea, yea; the woe consequent upon disobedience, the nay, nay, of the Godhead. These God daily speaketh to him whose eyes and ears are open. Other than these I have not heard. When, therefore, the life of man shall have been made to respond to the command which is in his being, giving the catholic result of a sound collective mind in a sound aggregate body, he will organize his human instrument or art for its human purpose, even as he shall have adapted his human life to the divine instrument which was given him. . . . There is no conceivable function which does not obey an absolute law. The approximation to that law in material, in parts, in their form, color and relations, is the measure of freedom of obedience to God, in life. . . . I call, therefore, upon science, in all its branches, to arrest the tide of sensuous and arbitrary embellishment, so far as it can do it, not negatively by criticism thereof alone, but positively by making the instrument a many-sided response to life. The craving for completeness will then obtain its normal food in results, not the opiate and deadening stimulus of decoration. Then will structure and its dependent sister arts emerge from the stand-still of *ipse dixit,* and, like the ship, the team, the steam-engine, proceed through phases of development towards a response to need.

But alas, though Greenough reached this exalted point, his mind, as though shaken by its own bold probings into philosophical vastnesses, began to lose its direction. Once before, when he was first in Rome, neglecting himself in his anxiety to learn and work, a severe attack of the "Roman fever" had left him with a temporarily clouded mind. Now, after all these years, his mind again began to wander. He was suddenly taken ill in the midst of delivering a course of lectures in Boston. He grew voluble and obscure, excitable, nervous, irritable, turning and passing from subject to subject. Mercifully the end was near.

If Greenough could have lived, clear-minded, to ripe old age (he died at forty-seven), lecturing, writing, and scattering his sound thoughts in American minds, perhaps some of the dreary stretches of the history of art in America in the latter half of the nineteenth century might have been different. Perhaps it is too much to expect that one man, with one idea of noble simplicity would have had any chance against the insensate tides of materialism which overwhelmed American art after the Civil War. Still, there is a possibility, had he lived, that we might have been spared instruction in "art applied to industry" from men like Walter Smith and Christopher Dresser, who were imported from the incredible depths of Victorian England to organize our art schools under the motto "Art Pays."

It is regrettable that Greenough realized too late that the important things he had to say could not be written in marble. It may seem that many of his years were wasted on sculpture, but it is doubtful that he could have reached his final ideas without some such apprenticeship at some craft.

After his death in 1852 Emerson wrote of him: "He was an accurate and deep man. He was a votary of the Greeks, and impatient of Gothic art. His paper on architecture, published in 1843, announced in advance the leading thoughts of Mr. Ruskin on the *morality* in architecture...."[49]

[49] Emerson, *English Traits*.

In another place Emerson says: "Our few fine persons are apt to die. Horatio Greenough, a sculptor, but whose tongue was far cunninger in talk than his chisel to carve, and who inspired great hopes, died two months ago at forty-seven ... I account that man, one product of American soil (born in Boston), as one of the best proofs of the capabilities of this country ..."[50]

In a prophetic moment Greenough wrote: "The man of vast power of mind is like the fortress full of armed hosts, with spears glittering over the turret, with pointed artillery and burning match. We sit down to sketch it and glorify it more cordially, when the portcullis chain is broken, the guns are spiked, and the ivy and the owl have possession of its towers."[51]

> Then mourn, my country! Shed
> Deep tears from thy great lids, and borrow
> Night's gorgeous gloom to deck thy sorrow;
> Greenough, thy son, is dead.
>
> GEORGE H. CALVERT, "Monody on the
> Death of Horatio Greenough"

[50] Emerson, Journal, Letter to Carlyle (1852).
[51] Greenough, [Essays] in H. J. Tuckerman, *Memorial of Horatio Greenough* (1853).

5 · GRAFFITTI D'IATLIA
or, Sketches of Florentine and Roman Art-Life

Though we travel the world over to find the beautiful, we must carry it with us, or we find it not.

RALPH WALDO EMERSON

By the time the American sculptors appeared on the Italian scene the neoclassic school was already on the decline. But the glowing legends clustering around the name of Canova, the Prince of Sculpture, and the precedents fixed by the English nobility for the manner of patronizing sculptors were set in an irresistibly powerful romantic pattern. In spite of all the precedents and patterns, however, there seemed to be a marked difference between the temper of the American and the English sculptors who lived as romantic exiles in the land of art. The Englishmen were much more likely to retain eighteenth-century ways of thinking about themselves and their art, whereas the Americans were less hampered by old-fashioned notions and traditions—*they* were men of the nineteenth century.

The English sculptors had fled from home to take up residence in Italy far from the cold and the encroachments of modern machines. John Gibson, the leading sculptor of the English colony in Rome, retained an eighteenth-century stage-coach frame of mind, even though he lived in the age of steam. He maintained, in his attitude toward his royal and noble patrons, an obsequious air that was totally foreign to the free-born Yankee artist. Gibson was never able to comprehend the mysterious scientific fact that railroads could not stop at selected inns or crossroads at the whim of the passenger. When he went back to visit in England he was forever getting off trains at wrong stations. In contrast, the different temper of American artists (even though they thought themselves just as "classical" as Gibson) is indicated in their reaction to the primitive methods of quarrying and moving blocks of marble at Carrara. One American artist, as soon as he arrived there wanted to organize a stock company and lay out a railroad to take the place of the oxen and men and women who tugged and strained to move heavy laden sledges.

It is reassuring to look at the products of the studios of European sculptors working at the same time and in the same style that was affected by our American artists, and there to find that the faults of American sculpture, which we might be inclined to consider as exclusively our own, were the faults of an age rather than the artistic fumblings of a young and provincial nation. The intense nationalists of the fabulous forties and the equally fabulous fifties managed to find all sorts of strictly American virtues in this sculpture which now seems to us to be all of a piece with the European sculpture of the time.

If their contemporaries are to be trusted, we are indeed dealing with an unusually gifted group of men—the critics and writers of the day all stress the diligence and elevated character of our classic sculptors. Almost all of them seem to have been exceptionally attractive personalities. Though many of them were men of little formal education they moved with ease among the scholars, statesmen, and literary men of their day. On migrating to Italy they mingled with cardinals, poets, and noblemen with a special early American complacency and pride. The intellectual and social circles of England and Italy received these noblemen from the exotic wildernesses of the New World with open arms. A tour of the studios of American sculptors became, by 1850, one of the accepted cultural duties of the annual winter tour of Italy. The glamorous studios were as much a part of the delightfully picturesque trip as doing the Florentine galleries and admiring the enchanting Roman ruins under the extraordinary blue Italian sky.

While thousands of emigrants were pouring into the United States and pushing ever westward into the wilderness, the sculptors were pioneers in reverse. They fled from the crude frontier, the "bright commercial newness" and the rapid changes of American life. They escaped from the vulgar false gentility of American society, and from the pushing social climbers and manufacturers and land speculators who were busy laying foundations for tremendous fortunes. The sculptors escaped to the secure permanency of a dead past in a decaying land.

The flight of the American artists to Art-Lands was considerably assisted in the 1840's by improved modes of travel. With the development of regular steamship schedules in the thirties and forties the trials and terrors of a transatlantic crossing were greatly reduced, and more and more people found the money and time to avail themselves of that cultural tone which could only be gained by a season abroad. Horatio Greenough recounts in a letter to his brother the pleasures of his crossing in the steamer "Great Western" in 1843:

Liverpool, Clayton Square
July 29, 1843

DEAR HARRY, — We have been three days here, and are convinced of the superiority of steamers to sailing ships. During the summer months at least. Not only have we escaped seasickness, but I can say without exaggeration that except for the inconvenience of a numerous company, and the stinted space afforded by our staterooms, we have been, as it were, in an agreeable hotel. You who know the sea life only as a sailor, can scarcely form an idea of the comfort of the "Great Western." No leaning to leeward, no ship odors, no thumping of blocks, etc. The responses of the waiters and the popping of the champagne corks are the only noises that call your attention. At night the handsome saloon, brilliantly lighted and filled with parties of whist, chess, and backgammon, presents a scene of gaiety seldom seen on shore.[1]

The ships on the return voyage from Italy were laden with marble passengers, sometimes with so much marble they ended their cruising for all time at the bottom of the sea. Hiram Power's statue of Calhoun helped drag down the ship in which Margaret Fuller and her husband and child were drowned off Fire Island. Though the statue was recovered Margaret was never found, and her manuscript on the Italian revolution was lost with them.

Some men seem, instinctively, to have chosen Florence as a place of study and residence rather than Rome. Apparently the presence in Florence of Hiram Powers and Horatio Greenough and others cast such a strong New England atmosphere over the City of Flowers that William Wetmore Story called it "a sort of continental Boston." But most of the men went to Rome to be near the galleries of antique sculpture, the immortal works of Canova, and the studios of Thorvaldsen and Gibson.

They reveled in the unaccustomed *dolce far niente* of the Roman Art Life at the same time accusing the easygoing Italians of "a want of moral earnestness." As if to make up for the Italian lack of earnestness, the Americans went to work studying, modeling, casting, copying, visiting museums and ruins with such vigor as to under-

mine their health, even to the point where the "old Roman fever" carried them off to leave their unmade masterpieces slumbering in the quarries at Carrara.

The impression which the first sight of Italy made upon the untutored backwoods Yankee sculptor fresh from a frontier town is most typically represented in a conversation of Hiram Powers, telling of his first trip to Rome:

On my first opportunity . . . Mr. Preston (an early patron of Powers) of South Carolina accompanied me in my visit to the galleries. He was so thoroughly read up and instructed, that he knew beforehand everything that he was going to see, and just where it was. But he was so impatient to get back to his family, that he hurried me through like lightning; and forgot that I had none of *his* careful culture and readiness to receive impressions at a glance. I have felt, on both my visits [to Rome], as if I were riding in an express-train through a canebrake, and was called upon to number the reeds. Rome oppresses me. It is crowded with wonders and artistic wealth, and yet so full of ruins and decay, that it seems to say, "What is the use of adding to this superfluity . . ." Florence was more than I could stand, when I first came out. My kind friends in America, who had persuaded themselves I was a young Michael Angelo, did not know how discouraged I felt by their extravagant praises, nor how dashed by the variety and extent of the sculpture I found here. "What can I add worthily," I said, "to these already countless treasures of art?" I believe I found more encouragement in finding some *bad* works in the galleries than in seeing the many *excellent* ones. They seemed to say, "Even bunglers may do things thought worthy of preservation." But Rome is a thousand times worse than Florence in this smothering accumulation of treasures. I could not live and preserve my own artistic independence and courage to labour and strive amid such an overwhelming crowd of artistic products . . .

Powers concludes by saying that he has no time to waste in going to Rome or even to America.[2]

By the middle of the century, Italy during the winter season was a melange of traveling tycoons, literary figures, and artists, both English and American—and among the travelers there was a generous sprinkling of English lords and Russian noblemen and serious German scholars. They basked in the warmth among the disparate fragments of the past. They moved from town to town in a glow of romantic historical associations. They wandered in galleries, stopping here and there to admire the fashionable masterpieces of Carlo Dolci and Guido

[1] F. B. Greenough, *Letters of Horatio Greenough* (1887).

[2] H. W. Bellows, *Seven Sittings with Powers the Sculptor* (1869).

Reni. They lived in vast apartments in moldering palaces under a dim heaven of blistered frescoes. They savored the noble Italian names almost as if they were edible and complained against the swarms of beggars, the universal dirt, and the inferior Italian political institutions.

There remained more or less constant among the flow of winter tourists the "romantic exiles"—the foreign artists. Among these there were a great many English and Germans, and, as the century wore on, more and more Americans. Beneath the glowing Italian sun our artists imagined themselves creating a new golden age of sculpture. Hawthorne—typically enough, but truly—detected something sinister in this haunting of tombs and ruins in a foreign land; it seemed to him unreal, unnatural. Like some other traveling Americans, he was oppressed by the dead burden of the past. But the exiled artists were like mice attracted to some noble old cheese by the very smell of its antiquity. They mistook the green mold of Italy's aged decay for a verdant springtime bower for themselves and for their art. They did not seem to realize as Hawthorne did that

The years, after all, have a kind of emptiness when we spend too many of them on a foreign shore. We defer the reality of life, in such cases, until a future moment, when we shall again breathe our native air; but, by and by, there are no future moments; or, if we do return, we find that the native air has lost its invigorating quality, and that life has shifted its reality to the spot where we have deemed ourselves only temporary residents. Thus between two countries we have none at all, or only that little space of either in which we finally lay down our discontented bones. It is wise therefore to come back betimes, or never.[3]

In Hawthorne's novel *The Marble Faun* and in his *Italian Note-Books* is preserved for us a wonderfully complete picture of the Art-Life (as it was then called) in Italy in 1858. He frequented the studios and salons of Rome and Florence, making shrewd observations on what he saw and heard there, and he recorded his private thoughts aroused by the busy events of the Roman season. For many years every American who went to Rome went armed with George Hillard's *Six Months in Italy* (1853), a book dedicated to Mr. and Mrs. Thomas Crawford, and when *The Marble Faun* was published (1860), these two books formed a really indispensable traveler's library—from them one could get the full flavor of the Italian Art-Life. It is indeed possible that the wide reading of Hawthorne's pungent criticisms of the neoclassic sculptors and their works may have contributed to the widespread neglect into which these American sculptors fell before the end of the century.

Hawthorne's remarks are valuable not only as a record of a curious phase of American art, but they are extremely interesting as the reactions of an intelligent man to the works and personalities of these exiles who were so loudly hailed as geniuses at home.

One of the reasons for the sculptors' romantic flight to Italy and also the basis for their active professional jealously is pointed out in *The Marble Faun:*

One of the chief causes that make Rome the favorite residence of artists—their ideal home which they sigh for in advance, and are loth to migrate from, after once breathing its enchanted air—is, doubtless, that they find themselves in force, and are numerous enough to create a congenial atmosphere. In every other clime they are isolated strangers; in this land of art, they are free citizens.

Not that . . . there appears to be any large stock of mutual affection among the brethren of the chisel and pencil. On the contrary, it will impress the shrewd observer that the jealousies and petty animosities which the poets of our day have flung aside, still irritate and gnaw into the hearts of this class of imaginative man. It is not difficult to suggest why this should be the fact. The public, in whose graces lie the sculptor's or the painter's prospects of success, is infinitely smaller than the public to which literary men make their appeal. It is composed of a very limited body of wealthy patrons; and these, as the artist well knows, are but blind judges in matters that require the utmost delicacy of perception. Thus success in art is apt to become partly an affair of intrigue; and it is almost inevitable that even a gifted artist should look askance at his gifted brother's fame, and be chary of the good word that might help him to sell still another statue or picture . . . a sculptor never has a favorable word for any marble but his own.

Nevertheless . . . artists are conscious of a social warmth from each other's company . . . They shiver at the remembrance of their lonely studios in the unsympathizing cities of their native land. For the sake of such brotherhood as they can find, more than from any good that they get from galleries, they linger year after year in Italy, while their originality dies out of them, or is polished away as a barbarism.[4]

For a scene in *The Marble Faun* that takes place in a sculptor's studio, Hawthorne describes for us the Roman

[3] *The Marble Faun.*

[4] *Marble Faun.*

studio of William Wetmore Story in the Via San Nicolo di Tolentino:

The studio of a sculptor is generally but a rough and dreary looking place, with a good deal the aspect, indeed, of a stone-mason's work-shop. Bare floors of brick or plank, and plastered walls; an old chair or two, or perhaps only a block of marble (containing, however, the possibility of ideal grace within it) to sit down upon; some hastily scrawled sketches of nude figures on the whitewash of the wall. These last are probably the sculptor's earliest glimpses of ideas that may hereafter be solidified into imperishable stone, or perhaps may remain as impalpable as a dream. Next there are a few very roughly modelled little figures in clay or plaster, exhibiting the second stage of the idea as it advances towards a marble immortality; and then is seen the exquisitely designed shape of clay, more interesting than the final marble, as being the intimate production of the sculptor himself, moulded throughout with his loving hands, and nearest to his imagination and heart. In the plaster cast, from this clay model, the beauty of the statue strangely disappears, to shine forth again with pure, white radiance, in the precious marble of Carrara. Works in all these stages of advancement, and some with the final touches upon them might be found in Kenyon's studio.[5]

Hawthorne continues to elucidate the mysteries of sculptors and sculpture, describing the method by which white marble took on human form—one cannot read this without suspecting that the author was having a sort of revenge on these pretentious geniuses when he so mercilessly exposes the secrets of their little game.

Here might be witnessed the process of actually chiseling the marble, with which (as it is not quite satisfactory to think) a sculptor, in these days has very little to do. In Italy, there is a class of men whose mere mechanical skill is perhaps more exquisite than was possessed by the ancient artificers, who wrought out the designs of Praxiteles; or, very possibly, by Praxiteles himself. Whatever of illusive representation can be effected in marble, they are capable of achieving, if the object be before their eyes. The sculptor has but to present these men with a plaster-cast of his design, and a sufficient block of marble, and tell them that the figure is embedded in the stone, and must be freed from its encumbering superfluities; and, in due time, without the necessity of his touching the work with his own finger, he will see before him the statue that is to make him renowned. His creative power wrought it with a word.

In no other art, surely, does genius find such effective instruments, and so happily relieve itself of the drudgery of actual performance; doing wonderfully nice things by the hands of other people, when it may be suspected they could not

[5] *Ibid.*

always be done by the sculptor's own. And how much of the admiration which our artists get for their buttons and button-holes, their shoeties, their neckcloths,—and these, at our present epoch of taste, take a large share of the renown,—would be abated, if we were generally aware that the sculptor can claim no credit for such pretty performances, as immortalized in marble! They are not his work, but that of some nameless machine in human shape.[6]

Frequently the sculptors worked all winter on their clay figures and busts, but when the heat and the dreaded Roman fever of summer came they turned over their clay studies to their workmen to "put them into marble," while the artist went off to explore some quaint hill town to escape from Rome. Sometimes they traveled in small groups, wandering over the mountains sketching, writing, and idling away the hot months until they could safely return to find their studies transformed from Tiber mud to glistening marble. It must have been a wonderful life.

In Rome the artists amused themselves between bouts of work by visiting the galleries and attending the more spectacular festivals of the Church. They wandered in bands at night through the moonlit ruins; they peopled the Coliseum with pathetic phantoms of early Christian martyrs. Sometimes parties were made up to tour the ruins in the dark of the moon, by the light of Bengal flares. Groups were organized at the English Bookshop in the Piazza di Spagna to tour the sculpture galleries of the Vatican at night by torchlight.

It is perhaps the most wonderful of your Roman experiences, to traverse those long galleries, pausing here and there amid the dark and silent shapes on either side, to throw the light of the torches upon some single figure, and behold it start, as it were, into being. The pale marble assumes a fleshy tint; the rigid limbs seem to relax, the eyes to move, the lips unclose; you see the hero or the matron of ancient days almost as their contemporaries saw them; you behold the god or goddess inspired with a life such as their worshippers of old never beheld, unless they, too, made their torchlight visits to the shrines of their divinities.[7]

Their sensations were excited by this "resurrection of the dead." They explored the Catacombs and rambled upon the Campagna, philosophizing, turning out bits of poetry, and talking of old times back home in the States.

[6] *Ibid.*
[7] S. Eliot, "Thomas Crawford," *American Quarterly Church Review and Ecclesiastical Register,* XI (April, 1858).

In Florence they dabbled in Spiritualism, attending seances where they questioned the spirits of the former inhabitants of the villas in which they lived. Some of the more sympathetic members of these circles experienced contacts with the dim spirit world which left them no doubt as to the genuineness of their adventures. The time-haunted atmosphere of Florence seemed particularly adapted to ghostly manifestations. Mrs. Hiram Powers declared that an ectoplasmic monk, materializing from some recess of her cozy drawing-room, had tugged at her skirts one evening so persistently that his other-worldly hand had quite ripped out the stitching.

At Mrs. Powers' "at homes" on Thursday evenings the fortunate guest was likely to meet any number of artists, painters, poets, and perhaps a stray Russian prince or an American millionaire looking for something suitable in the way of a piece of parlor statuary in Carrara marble to take home as a souvenir. Whereas in Rome, in the sumptuous suite of the Storys in the Palazzo Barberini, another similar group, though more brilliant and diverse in character, might be found. Perhaps the dear Brownings would be down from Florence for a visit—who could tell whom you might not meet. Mrs. Stowe might be there, or Hans Christian Andersen, or Thackeray, or Liszt, or even a Cabot. Perhaps the evening would be enlivened with a theatrical performance in William Story's private theatre with Tomasso Salvini, the great actor, playing some minor role in a drama from the facile pen of the sculptor.

If the tourists were not lucky enough to be invited to these evening parties, they at least had free access to the sculptors' studios in the daytime. They flowed in an endless stream; one sculptor boasts that in one day he had as many as four English lords all at one time. The latter were always popular visitors because of their casual way of ordering portrait busts and ideal figures in marble, a pleasant English custom quickly copied by American travelers ennobled by wealth newly gained.

The lives of the English sculptors who preceded the Americans to Italy by only a decade or two are strikingly parallel to those of our American geniuses. Many of them were not much better educated to begin with than the Americans, but their good fortune in getting commissions seemed to progress in the same way.

Not all the visitors to studios and evening parties were literary figures or millionaires or lords—some of them were merely social travelers—young bucks from England bent on having a good time—they tried every trick they could think of to get into a studio when a nude female was posing and caused no end of scandal and trouble. There were some awful, overbearing English tourists newly rich from the black manufacturing cities of the Midlands—it was not until some time later that one heard complaints of the vulgar American tourists.

Hawthorne says of the sculptors as a group:

It is fair to say, that they were a body of very dextrous and capable artists, each of whom had probably given the delighted public a nude statue, or had won credit for even higher skill by the nice carving of buttonholes, shoe-ties, coat-seams, shirt-bosoms, and other such graceful peculiarities of modern costume. Smart, practical men they doubtless were, and some of them far more than this, but, still, not precisely what an uninitiated person looks for in a sculptor. A sculptor indeed to meet the demand which our preconceptions make upon him, should be even more indispensably a poet than those who deal in measured verse and rhyme. His material or instrument, which serves him in the stead of shifting and transitory language, is a pure white undecaying substance. It insures immortality to whatever is wrought in it, and therefore makes it a religious obligation to commit no idea to its mighty guardianship, save such as may repay the marble for its faithful care, its incorruptable fidelity, by warming it with an ethereal life. Under this aspect marble assumes a sacred character; and no man should dare to touch it unless he feels within himself a certain consecration. . . .

No such ideas as the foregoing—no misgivings suggested by them—probably troubled the self-complacency of most of these clever sculptors. Marble, in their view, had no such sanctity as we impute to it. It was merely a sort of white limestone from Carrara, cut into convenient blocks, and worth in that state, about two or three dollars per pound; and it was susceptible of being wrought into certain shapes (by their own mechanical ingenuity, or that of artisans in their employment) which would enable them to sell it again at a much higher figure. Such men on the strength of some small knack in handling clay, which might have been fitly employed in making waxworks, are bold to call themselves sculptors. How terrible should be the thought, that the nude woman whom the modern artist patches together, bit by bit . . . shall last as long as the Venus of the Capitol! that his group—no matter what, since it has no moral or intellectual existence—will not physically crumble any sooner than the immortal agony of the Laocoön.[8]

The favorite argument that enlivened many an evening in the studios and salons of Florence and Rome was

[8] Hawthorne, *Marble Faun*.

whether marble in its purity or paint was the best means of expressing noble thoughts. The sculptors, of course, held that form and pure Carrara were infinitely superior —they were real, tangible, whereas a painting was actually a visual lie—a compound of illusions. John Gibson, the English sculptor, tried to solve the problem by tinting one of his marble Venuses; a dreadful mistake—even though the Greeks did paint their statues—it was no better than a waxworks. Some thought it a very daring bit of modernity, but to others it was too lewd and lifelike; in any case it was the sensation of the studios for months—three replicas were sold to English collectors as fast as Gibson could make them. He spent so much time contemplating his work the gossips began to call the Venus "Mrs. Gibson."

Another problem that troubled both painters and sculptors was what to do with the modern costume. Only a fool would think of carving a life-size statue of a woman in a hoop-skirt—think of how much marble it would take. The male costume posed another problem because it was plainly not at all picturesque. Some sculptors as we have seen, did not worry about the lack of beauty of modern clothing—they concentrated on the button-holes and minute details of tailoring to cover up the drab facts of breeches, waistcoats, stovepipe hats— others resorted to Greco-Roman nightgowns and togas— a plan which often led to ludicrous results.

The *Cosmopolitan Art Journal* says (in 1860), "American sculptors in Italy are representatives of a higher order of genius. Their studios are among the finest in Florence and Rome—their works are in constant demand—their society is sought by all classes, as men and women, they wield an influence which is very pleasant to contemplate. ... At this moment the estimation in which Mr. Powers, Mr. Hart, Mr. Ives, and Miss Hosmer, are held is such as to flatter our national vanity. . . ."[9]

On the other hand, Hawthorne says of his conversation with Mrs. Jameson (the author of *Sacred and Legendary Art*), "At any rate, she pronounced a good judgment on the American sculptors now in Rome, condemning them in the mass as men with no high aims, no worthy conception of the purpose of their art, and desecrating marble by the things they wrought in it. William Story, I presume, is not to be included in this censure ... On my part I suggested that the English sculptors were little or

nothing better than our own, to which she acceded generally ..."[10]

William Story, writing to James Russell Lowell in 1864, has much the same comment to make—"For the most part, and scarcely with an exception among the American artists, art is [here] but a money making trade, and I can have no sympathy with those who are artists merely to make their living."[11]

Even the critics, who had shouted "genius" most loudly and most often, began in the sixties to criticize our sculptors for living in the past—marking the beginning of the end of the neoclassic school. A foreign correspondent writes to the *Cosmopolitan Art Journal*:

With the eminent models before them, of the great masters, the student has a constant stimulus to great works. This, it seems to me, is a great and serious fault, for no artist thinks of anything but what was "high art" for its key. Many of the artists here, when at home, were admirable for delineation and spirit; but, from the presence of the great models; from the desire to emulate; from the criticisms of the Italians, who think nothing but Angelos and Raphaelles; from the very *presence* of the past, these worthy workers have lost much of their piquant and peculiar characteristics, and are gradually simulating to what is "Classical." Every original they attempt almost, is some classical subject. As if the Present, with its wonderful life and action—with tragedies, comedies, and melodramas, such as the ancient world never knew—was not fitted for delineation! Oh, this everlasting worship of the past is a great humbug! When will an artist learn to cope with the orator and poet by painting *to* the people? and cease to paint only *for* the learned?

One of the curiosities of the Yankee-Roman art world was a group of female sculptors from the States that appeared in the fifties, a direct result of the rising tides of feminism. The leader of this "white marmorean flock," as Henry James calls them, was Harriet Hosmer, a girl from Watertown, Massachusetts, who was perhaps the most talented of the lady sculptors—at least she had the greatest talent for making friends with influential people. She was the cause of much excitement because of her willful ways, which were, if unconventional for Boston, quite beyond belief for the Romans. She went everywhere unchaperoned, rode horseback astride, dissected corpses, and in general gave the already active tongues of gossip and scandal something to talk about. Another exotic was Edmonia Lewis, a girl of mixed American Indi-

[9] *Cosmopolitan Art Journal*, IV (Dec., 1860).

[10] *Note-Books.*
[11] Henry James, *William Wetmore Story and His Friends* (1903).

an and Negro blood—apparently her most striking claim to fame was the contrast of the color of her skin with the white marble in which she worked—at least that is what her contemporaries loved to remark upon. There were others too, for instance, there was Miss Emma Stebbins, a spinster, who took up sculpture at the age of forty-two and was irresistably drawn to the Roman "Art-Life." One of her most ambitious works, the *Angel of the Waters,* now graces a large fountain at the end of the Mall in Central Park, New York City. And then there was Miss Vinnie Ream (later Mrs. Hoxie), who as a gifted child of fifteen "shook saucy curls in the lobbies of the Capitol and extorted from susceptible senators commissions for national monuments."[12]

But the artist's flight to sunny Italy was not all romance and classical art; entwined in the heart of the sumptuous garland of "art-life" in Florence and Rome ran a very practical sustaining thread—one that any Yankee could take hold of and understand and one that appealed most nearly to the heart of the "business artists," as Jarves called them. It was the "celestial cheapness"—the very low cost of living in Italy—that charmed them all, along with the Venus de Medici and the treasures of the Vatican. The Reverend Henry Bellows asked Hiram Powers how important he thought it for American artists to come abroad. Hiram's answer is so revealing it must be given at length; as you will see art and the artistic advantages of a residence in Italy are scarcely mentioned—it was merely a practical matter of cost. Hiram said,

A landscape painter may remain at home . . . But sculpture is universal. The human form is of no country, and may be studied with equal advantage at home and abroad. The opportunities of studying it abroad are so immeasurably greater than at home, that I don't see how it is possible, without great loss, to neglect them.

1. It is impossible to model successfully without living models; and in America, in my time, it was almost at the peril of reputation, both for model and sculptor, that the artist employed the living model even if he could procure it. . . . [models can be secured now in New York but they are rare and expensive—$2 and $3 per day] . . . whereas they are only 80 cents in Italy . . . [here Powers philosophizes on the sad lot of professional models] . . . I shrink from the responsibility of leading anyone into so perilous a vocation.

2. Opportunities here of anatomical studies are nearly perfect, and free of all expense. The medical schools . . . are open to all artists . . . [This indispensible training] can only be obtained in America at great cost.

3. Marble is no cheaper here than in New York, the transportation costs from Carrara are the same *but* good workmen who cannot be dispensed with, are so abundant and so cheap here, and so rare and so dear at home that it alone is a decisive reason for coming abroad . . . [Powers pays his best workman at the rate of $4 per day] . . . He could make twice that cutting weeping willows on American tombstones . . . I employ a dozen workmen in my studios . . . The whole costs me about fifteen dollars per day, which is wonderfully low . . . my rent [is] only about four hundred and fifty dollars annually.

4. The general expenses of maintaining a family are so much less here than at home . . . [an artist] . . . finds an immense inducement to live abroad . . . [Other than music and languages the educational opportunities are not good for children.] There are, however, less temptations to vice, and less exposure to the American habit of hard drinking among young men; but, no doubt, the general influences here in the way of developing a manly, energetic and self-reliant character, are less favorable than at home. There is . . . a want of moral earnestness in Italy . . . On the other hand, the money-getting propensities and social rivalries of America tend to harden human character, and bring out a severe selfishness . . . [but] American youth are better brought up in America. But the artist must make this sacrifice to his art . . . most sculptors lose individuality both at home and abroad . . .[13]

In spite of the parties, the pleasurable excitement of a flow of commissions, the social and economic and artistic advantages offered by life in Italy, all our romantic exiles seem to have been troubled with twinges of homesickness, subconsciously they seemed to realize the falseness of their position and to long for home. Their letters are full of such remarks as these: "This Florence is a dirty old place when it rains; but when the sun is out nothing can be more charming—excepting Boston."

One sculptor's wife, writing from Florence to her mother in Boston, says, "We have not finished the "Transcripts" yet, as we take them out but one a day in the order of their dates . . . It is laughable to hear him ask for 'today's paper.' I don't think anything seems more homelike than to see him sit down to his "Transcript" after dinner."[14] A sculptor writes, "The Cabots have gone to Rome. I made a bust of Madam C. . . . Mr. Cabot reminded me of old times, his face is so reminiscent of State Street." And in another place "Two sisters of Count R. . . . have been here; they are just like our best Bostonians."[15]

The neoclassic lingerers in Rome had no good word to say for "modern" art (1880–90). Impressionism was

[12] James, *William Wetmore Story and His Friends.*

[13] Bellows, *Seven Sittings* . . .
[14] Mrs. Thomas Ball.
[15] Greenough.

anathema, and the extreme realism of the Academy was no less crude and annoying to the men who had been cradled so long in the cocoon of classic convention. One of them voices his displeasure thus, "The modern school has done one good thing for Art, in letting in day-light to their studios . . . One of the evils of this broad light would seem to be the discovery and development of all the most hideous phases of nature that had been hitherto concealed or ignored as unworthy of Art . . . Purity has had her day; it's time she retired, and made room for nightmares and nastiness."[16]

ON THE DEATH OF AN AMERICAN SCULPTOR[17]
by Mrs. Lydia H. Sigourney (1860)

'Tis not for song to give thee fame,
　　O artist! praised by all,
For breathing marble guards thy name
　　In many a lordly hall;

[16] Thomas Ball.
[17] "Edward Sheffield Bartholomew, 1822–1858," *Cosmopolitan Art Journal*, IV, No. 1 (Mar., 1860), 5.

Yet tender Friendship's lambent lay
　　May trace thy varied lot
For those who saw thee day by day
　　And understood thee not;

Nor marked the new-fledged eagle's pain
　　That, fired with sunward trust,
Intensely struggled with the chain
　　That darkly bound to dust.

But, musing on thy glorious power
　　Thus quenched in early years,
We mourn thee in our secret bower
　　With stifled sound of tears,

And more than all thy loss to Art,
　　The pride of Freedom's shore,
We mourn the noble, loving heart
　　That beats for us no more.

6 · THE INGENIOUS YANKEE MECHANIC
or, The Statuary Business

The Popes have long been the patrons and preservers of art, just as our new, practical Republic is the encourager and upholder of mechanics. In their Vatican is stored up all that is curious and beautiful in art; in our Patent Office is hoarded all that is curious and useful in mechanics. When a man invents a new style of horse-collar or discovers a new and superior method of telegraphing, our government issues a patent to him that is worth a fortune; when a man digs up an ancient statue in the Campagna, the Pope gives him a fortune in gold coin. We can make something of a guess at a man's character by the style of nose he carries on his face. The Vatican and the Patent Office are Governmental noses, and they bear a deal of character about them.

Mark Twain, Innocents Abroad

IN an age of notable scientific advance and mechanical invention it seemed as if the time spirit, in its exuberance, overflowed into all departments and phases of life. The vocabulary of science and machinery colored the arts of the times, turning up in the most unexpected places—in the novels of George Eliot for instance, or in the romantic recesses of a young American sculptor's studio in Florence. The strong mechanical turn in the personalities of our sculptors is apparent not only in the variety of actual mechanical inventions they contrived and patented, but also in their sculptural works. In the methods by which these works were turned out in quantity, the machine and mechanical ways of thinking overshadowed almost everything but a pallid eclectic glimmer of classical mythology.

While many ingenious Americans were busy in the nineteenth century inventing practical machines for the mass production of tacks or gunstocks or textiles or fanciful gadgets for paring apples—to lighten labor and create all kinds of commercially valuable goods—the sculptors were busy in the studios of Florence, Rome, Albany, and Cincinnati confecting "machines" of marble, whose products—though consisting of the intangibles of melancholy sentiment and vanity—were nonetheless eminently desirable commodities.

The sculptors assembled artful marble machines, that in turn manufactured an aura of "art-culture" in many a cluttered Victorian parlor. These works of art could bring a heaving sigh to the bosom, a tear to the eye of a generation given to easy emotional responses. The art lovers were conditioned to react in a certain way to a compound of white marble and classical mythology, just like Dr. Pavlov's dogs that drooled at the sound of a bell. It was a matter of course if a grown man burst into tears on being told that his sculpture was beautiful. A work of art in white marble could positively hypnotize. For example, Hiram Powers' *Greek Slave* drew forth the following effusion from a female art critic.

In 1847 this statue was brought to America and placed on exhibition in the National Academy [of Design], Broadway, New York. Shrieks of admiration began to ring through the papers, and we repaired to the spot to see what these sudden outcries meant.

As we entered, we found ourselves in a new world, and a new atmosphere such as we had never breathed before. The Slave stood on a revolving pedestal, about four feet high. The light fell on it from the sky window. Seats were placed in front of it, into one of which we sank in a sort of trance, repeating audibly to the ear of our soul—

"A thing of beauty is a joy forever!"

. . . The history of her fallen country, her Greek home, her Greek lover, her Greek friends, her capture, her exposure in the public marketplace; the freezing of every drop of her young blood beneath the libidinous gaze of shameless traffickers in beauty; the breaking up of the deep waters of her heart; their calm settling down over the hopeless ruins, flowed noiselessly into the rapt ear of our mind. Voices from a group near roused us from our stupor, when we found we had been in this spell for five hours.[1]

As a machine for generating a sentimental daze the *Greek Slave* was indeed a huge success.

References to machines seemed to run through the thoughts of everyone. The Reverend Henry Bellows says of Powers, "His remarkable eyes, not second to Daniel Webster's . . . see forms, whether of thoughts or things, in precise outline, and his hand, an exquisite machine when Nature moulded it, has developed all its hidden cunning, until it matches his eye perfectly. I have never seen any mechanic work with more calm confidence at his trade than Powers works at his art."[2]

[1] Anna G. Lewis.
[2] Bellows, *Seven Sittings . . .*

Hawthorne calls the Italian marble workers "nameless machines in human form." Powers castigates the German sculptor Schwanthaler by calling him a machine for the production of statues and busts. Some studio visitors of the day, in a typically American hurry to see themselves or their children immortalized in marble, consider the sculptors as little more than machines. Greenough complains that they seem to think that busts and ideal figures could be turned out "like so many yards of sheeting." Hiram Powers speaks for the mechanic tribe when he says in a letter to his patron, Nicholas Longworth, in Cincinnati: "You know my love of mechanics. It was one of my earliest affections, and I have never been weaned from the *mother* which supported me before I knew anything of sculpture. Some of my happiest hours were spent in Watson's Clock Factory, and in my little workshop in Dorfeuill's [sic] Museum, and here, during the 20 years we have been abroad, I have devoted many an evening . . . to mechanical contrivances, and I have invented several improvements which I think would pay well if exploited."[3]

Many of the sculptors went a significant step further in indicating their subconscious conception of sculpture as "machinery" or "invention"—salable property in need of legal protection—by having their sculpture patented, going through all sorts of complicated legal procedures and expense, filing papers in the Patent Office to protect their designs from reproduction. Thomas Ball patented his design for a bust of Jenny Lind[4] but soon found the patent no protection at all. Because there was such a demand for Jenny, the bust was soon "pirated" and turned out in quantity by commercial competitors in New York. All of the famous Rogers Groups are patent statuary.

"Ingenious mechanician" was, in 1850, a tribute from critical flattery to the "grecian genius" in sculpture. As we have seen, almost every American sculptor invented something mechanical—and his marble Slaves and Junos were rather indiscriminately called "inventions," too. It enraged the sculptors to have their works copied and sold, though they spent their lives stealing ideas from the ancient sculptors in the galleries of the Vatican. In the biography of Leonard Volk we read:

While his attention was almost entirely given, for weeks, to the Art Gallery of the last of the two Sanitary Fairs (1865) . . .

a great demand suddenly sprung up all over the country for plaster copies of his bust of Lincoln, who had just been assassinated. He trusted the business of supplying the demand to employees, and consequently failed to realize as much out of it as he should have done. Parties in New York and elsewhere, also infringed his patent by duplicating the bust—the same thing that was attempted in Chicago by itinerant Italian image vendors, in 1861, when Mr. Volk, "taking the law into his own hands," entered their shop and broke to pieces all their moulds and casts, for which they prosecuted him for "trespass," and finally for "riot," but, failing to get satisfaction, have since carefully avoided an infringement upon his rights or property.[5]

Jarves says, "It is unnecessary to allude by name to the crowd of common sculptors, of whom America already has an ample supply. These men degrade art to a trade. They manufacture statuary on the same principle that they would make patent blacking, founding their standard of success on the amount of their sales. And yet their work is not to be altogether condemned, mechanical and lifeless as it may be, because it helps to familiarize the public with the idea of art, and gradually creates a desire for something better."[6]

In August 1842 patents for design were first authorized by the third section of a Patent Act.[7] The official Gazette of the United States Patent Office,[8] stating the object of the design act, says it is "to encourage works of art and decoration which appeal to the eye, to the aesthetic emotions, and to the beautiful."

The number of patents issued for sculpture, beginning in 1843, rises slowly to a peak in 1865, when twenty-two monuments, busts, and statuettes were patented. Among the artists in our group, John Rogers, Thomas Ball, Franklin Simmons, and Leonard Volk regularly patented their designs while working in the United States.

The other holders of sculpture patents represent a host of lesser men. In 1865 no less than eight busts, three medallions, one monument, and one statuette, all of Abraham Lincoln, were patented, most of them by men

[3] "Letters of Hiram Powers to Nicholas Longworth," *Quarterly Publications of the Historical and Philosophical Society of Ohio,* I (1906).
[4] Patented 1851.
[5] *Biographical Sketches of the Leading Men of Chicago* (1868).
[6] Jarves, *The Art Idea.*
[7] The third section of the Patent Act of 1842 reads, in part, as follows: "And be it further enacted, that any citizen . . . who by his or her or their own industry, genius, effort, and expense may have invented or produced any new and original design for manufacture . . . or any new and original design for a bust, statue, or bas-relief, or composition in baso-relievo . . . not known or used by others before his or her or their own invention or production thereof, and prior to the time of his . . . application for a patent therefor, and who shall desire to obtain an exclusive property or right therein to make, use, sell and vend the same . . . may make application in writing to the Commissioner of Patents, and the Commissioner . . . may grant a patent therefor . . . the duration of said patent shall be seven years . . ." (William Shoemaker, *Patents for Designs . . .* Washington, 1929.)
[8] Issue no. 1286.

whose names are never found in histories of American Art. In 1842 a patent was issued to L. Myers of Philadelphia for his invention of a method of casting statues. That same year the sculptor Henry Dexter received a patent for a "sculptor's apparatus." In 1849 the well-known Connecticut woodcarver and sculptor Hezekiah Augur patented a carving machine. In 1851 a patent for a carving machine was granted to a Mr. Charles Starr, and in 1852 a carving machine invented by Charles Bacon of Buffalo, New York, received a patent. Between 1790 and 1847 no less than eighteen devices of one sort or another for polishing, cutting, or sawing marble were patented.

The sculptors gave embodiment to political symbols for legislators and made parlor statues and portrait busts for the business man. As a return for this attention to national need and personal vanity, the politicians and business men gave sculptors, in design patents, the kind of property protection that they most valued themselves. The design patent Act of 1842 is one of the earliest governmental efforts toward the encouragement of the arts in America.

Early in the century clever Yankee inventors discovered the road to mass production through the manufacture of machines with interchangeable parts. The idea was in the air. It was a monumentally simple though revolutionary concept, destined to bring about the most extraordinary changes. The sculptors busied themselves applying to sculpture the discoveries of their fellow mechanics and successful business men. The secrets of John Rogers' success were popular subject matter chosen with a showman's instinct, mechanical mass production methods, legal protection for his property rights by design patents, low manufacturing costs, wide advertising, and mail-order distribution. John Rogers and his immortal groups typify the nineteenth-century mechano-sculptural synthesis in its most successful phase—what sculptor before him had sold 100,000 examples of his work? Though, strictly speaking, sculpture was not made with interchangeable parts, it might as well have been. In 1875 Jarves wrote in *Art Thoughts*:

If ... [art's] ... highest purpose was only to exhibit form, distance, proportion, local color and the physical relation of things in detail and mass, then any instrument which could measure sufficiently and take in enough points, could do the artistic work, or the most of it ... Can we compose beauty by mathematical receipt? ... Yet there are artists who claim that this is the true and final rule of art; a delusion which even their own inept productions do not dispel. I do not refer to the conscientious painters ... but of that delusion, chiefly confined to sculpture, which comes of the proclivity of the American mind to mechanics. In thus speaking of the mechanical and commercial spirit of American artists, it is not that I do not highly value trade and mechanics, but because their virtues, if applied dominantly to art, become its vices ... Machine work is the one great idealism of our prosaic civilization. Even Story, whose artistic cultivation ought to preserve him from such an error, advocates in his treatise on proportion in sculpture, the adoption of a formula by which he claims he can repeat the feat of Telekles and Theodorus, artists who wrought so perfectly by rule, that the half of a Pythian Apollo was made by one at Samos, and the other half at Ephesus by his companion, the halves fitting when brought together, as precisely as if the statue had been the work of one hand. If this mechanical success of parts were the true aim of art, we should establish separate manufactories of statues in pieces, as of watches, to be put together as needed, with extra members warranted to fit in case of loss of any of the first set.[*]

Joel Hart, the Kentucky master, invented a pointing machine for making busts that was so complicated none of the other Yankee geniuses in Italy could be induced to use it. But a small advertisement in a London paper brought Hart many commissions for portrait bursts from ladies and gentlemen anxious for the modern distinction of being "done" by machinery.

Thomas Blanchard, a Massachusetts man, was the inventor of one of the most important machines conceived during the early nineteenth century. He invented a lathe for the reproduction of irregular forms—invented to make gun-stocks and shoe lasts. The value of this machine was very great and it was put to many uses. Blanchard took one of his lathes to Washington to demonstrate its unique qualities to senators and congressmen in 1820 in order to get it patented.

To show what his machine could do in the way of reproducing irregular forms he caused the busts of several prominent legislators to be carved with it in wood from plaster models. "He turned the heads of Congress," the wits said. The congressmen were properly impressed with this remarkable exhibition of American ingenuity and they granted him his patent and gave him some government work to do. The "sculpture" Blanchard produced for this demonstration has long since disappeared.

[*] Jarves, *Art Thoughts* (1869).

In 1855 Mr. Blanchard took his machine to the Exposition Universelle in Paris to show off his invention and see the sights of Europe. The machine was the mechanical wonder of the Exposition.[20] Sculptors who made their living by doing portrait busts flocked to stand in awe and fear before this automatic monster that seemed to threaten their means of livelihood. Some of them declared that thenceforth sculpture was dead, forgetting that, in spite of the marvelous ingenuity of the machine, it could not create its own original patterns to copy. As the painters a few years before had feared that painting had come to an end with the invention of the daguerreotype, so did the sculptors tremble and fulminate at this fascinating and horrible machine which turned out before their eyes endless copies of busts of Napoleon III and the Empress Eugenie, automatically reducing and enlarging with unerring precision. Blanchard had by that time made a number of improvements on his machine and now it would carve marble as well as wood. The French public was so enamored of the machine that they claimed Blanchard as a Frenchman. The threat of the machine to the sculptors failed to materialize, however, and evidently it never gave them half the competition they exepected.

Thus, while professional sculptors were busy with mechanical contrivances, we have Mr. Blanchard, a professional mechanic and inventor, playing with sculpture as a mechanical tour de force. The confusion of sculpture and machinery seemed to be a part of the pattern of the time. There was, during the nineteenth century, a sort of restless inventive play with machines, back and forth among the three dimensions, which is reflected in the art of the time. There was a curious mixture of machinery, waxworks, sculpture, and theatrical fustian entangled with the endeavor to produce the illusion of reality via the machine. We have the sculpture of the lathe, the mass production methods of industry applied to the statuary business, the stereoscopic photograph, the moving panorama, and the automata of the waxworks, not to mention the "sun paintings" of Daguerre. The sculpture of the time has a machine-like precision of surface "giving the appearance of minute and protracted labour" though in reality produced quickly by mechanical means. The more theatrical sculpture of the day gives the impression of waxworks automata that have ceased to function because their clockwork mechanism has got out of kilter.

[20] Catalogue No. 144, Class VI, Section 6 (Annexe).

They are no longer able to move either themselves or the spectator. One can no longer be sure that the majority of these creations are sculpture—perhaps they are merely outmoded machines which have developed the same nostalgic charm that we see in an old-fashioned steam engine. Certainly no one ever discovers in the sculpture of the time any whit of the formal functional elegance of the clipper ship. But it is to be remembered that the ship was the creation of craftsmen rather than mechanics.

There will be little argument that most of the creations of American sculptors who grew to maturity before the Civil War are but feeble examples of the plastic art. Too often in their works intention outruns skill, structure is sacrificed to sentiment and surface, form is engulfed in literary embellishment, and melodrama makes mockery of vigor. Artistically they are but minor triumphs. They offer a permanent proof that the sculptors from the American frontier were for the most part bemused by a romantic synthesis of myths, marble, and machines. With little or no education, with no early training in art, they could only grasp at the merest superficialities of the difficult art of sculpture. However, one must not forget that European sculptors of the same time, with all the artistic advantages in their favor, could do little better than their American rivals.

None of them had the advantage that Praxiteles and Phidias had—that of believing in the gods and goddesses they found embedded in stone. However, the things the American sculptors did believe appear in their works more and more plainly as time passes. As we have seen, they were men sensitive to the ideals and influences of their time. They lived in an era of progress and eclecticism, of vulgarity and reform, of romance and machines. It was a time of rapid, too rapid, industrial expansion checkered with financial panics and depressions. The triumphant materialism of the day was all powerful, it quickly twisted the stark Asiatic grandeur of Emerson's Transcendentalism to its own mercenary ends, and under its influence the art of sculpture in the hands of ingenious Yankee mechanics became, by popular demand, the "statuary business." The sculptors were geniuses in a hurry, they were mechanical tinkerers through whom the immemorial human urge to create images found release in an age of romantic sentiment and machines. In their works are to be found the sins and virtues of that age petrified in dazzling Carrara. Though artistically their point of departure was the fading Olympus of an untenable classicism, their destination was the bleak uncompromising realism of Monument Square in almost any American town. They rode to fame on the triumphant machines of their time, and fell, responsive victims, to every current belief and ideal. Artistic success was to them a matter of sales volume rather than understanding of their chosen craft. Their "inventions" were enshrined, "protected from infringement" in the files of the Patent Office in Washington—the American Parthenon, a temple of gadgets and ingenuity. Though their cumbersome creations do not reflect as minutely the intellectual climate of their day as do the written works of the period, their contribution to American life is a tangible record in plaster and marble of the form of their time.

From the very earliest times there has been a powerful interest in and curiosity about machines in human form. In the nineteenth century the interest in the machine began to overpower the ancient interest in the human symbol. This has resulted, in the present century, in the total discard of the human symbol by artists of some schools in favor of abstract "art machines." Lewis Mumford calls this "the katharsis of art by the machine." The symbolic accumulations of centuries have by this katharsis been scientifically dissolved away from the fundamental framework of functional form to leave us free to create new symbols suitable for modern purposes. In the main, the sculpture of the nineteenth century represents, then, a phase of this transition.

But balanced against the patented soldiers' monument and tons of repetitive parlor statuary stand the faithful portraits of some of our greatest national heroes, a scant half dozen pieces of sculpture by William Rimmer, and the creative ideas of Horatio Greenough. What does it matter that most of our sculptors lost their way in a maze of machines to end in the "statuary business," if one of them strikes through the labyrinth to a truly significant idea. Though Greenough's sculpture is, naturally, characteristic of his time, his ideas have for us a modern ring. Though caught in the toils of the machine age no less

than his fellow artists, where they saw its advantages for turning sculpture into an industry, he caught a deeper meaning from the confusion of standards that the machine had introduced.

He approached his remarkable idea somewhat fumblingly at first; in a letter to Emerson he sets down roughly his thought, "Here is my theory of structure: a scientific arrangement of spaces and forms to function and to site; an emphasis of features proportioned to their *gradated* importance in function; color and ornament to be decided and arranged and varied by strictly organic laws, having a distinct reason for each decision; the entire and immediate banishment of all make-shift and make-believe."[11] Later his ideas solidify into a simple formula. In his little book, *Travels, Observations, and Experiences of a Yankee Stonecutter*, published in 1852 under the penname of Horace Bender, we find the "Stonecutter's Creed":

Three proofs do I find in man that he was made only a little lower than the angels—Beauty—Action—Character.

By beauty I mean the promise of function.
By action I mean the presence of function.
By character I mean the record of function.

Here is adumbrated the prime fundamental of functional design which has so powerfully affected all phases of modern life, our ways of thinking, no less than our arts, our homes, and all industrial design.

Perhaps in furnishing Greenough with a pedestal composed of countless mechanical marbles from which he could glimpse the true significance of science and the machine to art, our ingenious Yankee mechanic sculptors have performed their best work. If all the melancholy marbles by the American sculptors of the Classico-Jacksonian school were burned to mordant lime and their few bronzes forged to other forms, this important idea which one of them plucked from a welter of trivialities would perhaps constitute their most remarkable and enduring monument.

[11] Emerson, *English Traits.*

PART II

The First American School of Sculpture

I · THE PRECURSORS

THE following list shows the crafts, trades, and traditions which form the occupational background from which the first American school of sculpture emerged. No special effort has been made to include here all of the many woodcarvers—particularly the carvers of ship's figureheads, who have been fully treated in *American Figureheads and Their Carvers,* by Pauline A. Pinckney (New York, 1940).

ALLEN, G., stonecutter, carver; active Boston 1716.

ANDREI, GIOVANNI (1770–1824), sculptor, Italian; born Carrara; active Washington.

AUGUR, HEZEKIAH (1791–1858), woodcarver, sculptor, inventor; New Haven.

BINON, sculptor, French; active Boston 1820.

BOWEN, DANIEL (1766–?), wax modeler; active Boston and Philadelphia 1790–1800.

BROOKS, SAMUEL, medalist; active Boston 1790.

BROWERE, JOHN H. I. (1792–1834), plasterworker, modeler; New York.

BUDD, EDWARD (?–1674), stonecutter, carver; Boston.

CAPELLANO, ANTONIO, sculptor, Italian; active United States 1815–27.

CARDELLI, GEORGIO (1791–?), sculptor, Italian; born Florence; active United States 1816–?

CARDELLI, PETER, sculptor, Italian; active United States c.1816–?

CAUSICI, ENRICO, sculptor, Italian; active United States c.1820–?

CERRACCHI, GIUSEPPE (c.1740–c.1801), sculptor, Italian; born Rome; died Paris; active United States 1791–98.

CHEVALIER, AUGUSTIN, sculptor, French?; active Baltimore c.1820–30.

CODNER, WILLIAM, stonecutter; active Boston 1742.

COFFEE, THOMAS, sculptor, English; active Charleston, S. C., c.1821–51?

COFFEE, W. J., sculptor, English; active New York c.1816–?

COGDELL, JOHN STEVENS (1778–1847), amateur sculptor, modeler; Charleston.

DIXEY, JOHN (senior) (?–1820), sculptor; born Dublin; active New York.

ECKSTEIN, JOHN (1750–c.1817), sculptor, German; Philadelphia.

ECKSTEIN, FREDERICK (1787–c.1835), sculptor, German; Cincinnati (son of John).

FRANZONI, CARLO (1786–1819), sculptor, Italian; born Florence; died Washington.

FRANZONI, GIUSEPPE, sculptor, Italian; came to United States c.1806.

FRAZEE, JOHN (1790–1852), stonecutter, sculptor; born Rahway, N. J.; died Compton, N. J.

GEYER, HENRY CHRISTIAN, stonecutter, plasterworker, German?; active Boston 1760–70.

GOTT, JOHN (1785–1860); active Albany, N.Y.?

GUION, DAVID, stonecutter, French?; active Cincinnati c.1830–40.

IARDELLA, GIUSEPPE, stonecutter, Italian; active Philadelphia c.1790.

KNIGHT, RICHARD (born c.1680–90), carver; active Boston.

LUPTON, MRS. FRANCES, sculptor, painter; active New York 1826–34?.

McINTIRE, SAMUEL (1757–1811), woodcarver, sculptor; born Salem, died Boston.

MILLER, GEORGE M., sculptor, German?; active United States 1790–1818?.

MORSE, S. F. B. (1791–1872), painter, inventor, modeler; born Charlestown, Mass.; executed one piece of sculpture; died New York.

MOULTHROP, REUBEN (1763–1814), painter, wax modeler; East Haven, Conn.

NORTHRUP, R. F., carver; active Hartford c.1830.

PARK (the Park family), carvers; active Boston late 18th century.

PERISCO, LUIGI, sculptor; active Washington c.1820–30.

PETTRICH, FRIEDRICH AUG. FERD. (1798–1872), sculptor; born Dresden; died Rome; active United States 1835–58 (itinerant).

PROVINI, carver; active Philadelphia 1796.

RAUSCHNER, JOHANN C. (1760–?), wax modeler; born Frankfurt; active Salem and Boston 1809–10.

REDIN, HENRY, carver; active Boston 1714.

ROBINSON (1658–?), carver; born Boston (father).

ROBINSON (1680–?), carver; born Boston 1680 (son).

RUSH, WILLIAM (1756–1833), sculptor, carver; Philadelphia.

SARTORI, GIOVANNI, sculptor, Italian; active Philadelphia c.1794.

SKILLIN, SIMEON (1716–78), carver; Boston.

STAGI, PIETRO, sculptor, Italian; active Philadelphia 1795–99.

VALAPERTI, sculptor, Italian; active Washington 1816?–1824?

WELCH, JOHN (1680/90–?), carver; born Boston.

WELLS, MRS. RACHEL, wax-modeler; active Philadelphia late 18th century; sister of Patience Wright.

WILLARD, SOLOMON (1783–1826), carver, stonecutter, architect, inventor, teacher; Boston.

WRIGHT, ELIZABETH, wax-modeler; daughter of Patience Wright.

WRIGHT, JOSEPH, wax-modeler; son of Patience Wright.

WRIGHT, PATIENCE (1725–86), wax-modeler; born Bordentown, N. J.; died London.

2 · A BIOGRAPHICAL DICTIONARY

AKERS, BENJAMIN PAUL (1825–61) was born in Saccarappa, Maine, the son of a lumber-mill owner. He was educated in Norwich, Connecticut. For a while he worked for his father, and invented a machine for making shingles. Later he went to Portland, Maine, to become a printer. Here he began to study painting. He saw, for the first time, a marble bust (the work of Edward A. Brackett, *q.v.*) which inspired in him the desire to become a sculptor. At twenty-four (1849), he went to Boston to learn from Joseph Carew the art of making plaster casts. With this slight training he returned to Portland and opened a studio jointly with a portrait painter. Here he executed a number of busts, among them those of Longfellow and John Neal. In 1851 he was enabled to go to Italy, where he received some instruction from Hiram Powers. The following year he returned to the United States and during the winter of 1853 was in Washington "taking" the portraits of Edward Everett, Sam Houston, and President Pierce. In 1855 he returned to Italy—"he felt he belonged in Rome"—and began to produce his best-known works: *Una and the Lion, St. Elizabeth of Hungary,* and *The Dead Pearl Diver.* In 1856 he traveled extensively in Europe and returned to the United States because of poor health. After another trip to Italy, he returned to Portland, again in bad health, in 1860. He married the poetess Mrs. Elizabeth Chase Taylor in Portland, and on the advice of his physician, he spent the winter in Philadelphia, finally succumbing there to tuberculosis in the early spring of 1861, aged thirty-six. Paul Akers was the author of a number of papers on art published in the *Crayon* and in the *Atlantic Monthly.* At his death his widow composed a memorial ode "Violet-Planting," which closes:

> Lo! with your blossoms his loved grave shall be
> Blue as the marvelous sea
> Laving the borders of his Italy!

AMES, SARAH FISHER (1817–1901) was born at Lewes, Delaware. Little seems to have been recorded about her life and work. She married the portrait painter Joseph Ames. Her portrait bust of Abraham Lincoln, which she patented in 1866, is now in the Capitol at Washington. She is known to have studied art in Boston and in Rome. She died in Washington, D. C., at the age of ninety-four.

ANDREWS, J. A. (active 1865), Patentee—Soldiers Monument, 1865.

ANNABLE, GEORGE OLIVER (c. 1829–1887) was born in Providence, R. I., the son of a cobbler. He was trained as a stonecutter and marble worker at the stoneyard of Mr. Tingley in Providence. In 1851 and 1853 he won prizes or medals for his cameo portraits and busts at the exhibitions of the Rhode Island Society for the Encouragement of Domestic Industry. He made busts of General Greene and Dr. Wayland and others and from these commissions made enough money to enable him to achieve his dream of going to Europe to study painting. He studied with Rothermel in Paris and with Page in Rome, staying in Europe for four years. As a painter he was not successful and apparently sculpture no longer attracted him; in any case he made no mark in either art. He died in Brooklyn, New York, when he was about fifty-eight years old.

ARMSTRONG, J. S. (active 1866–67), Patentee—Military Monuments, 1866 and 1867.

BAILLY, JOSEPH ALEXIS (1825–83) was born in Paris, the son of a cabinetmaker. He was trained as a woodcarver and worked in his father's shop. In the Revolution of 1848 he was conscripted against his will and managed to escape to the United States. For a time he worked in New Orleans but finally settled in Philadelphia, where he soon became a leading figure in the art circles of the city. He remained in Philadelphia for the rest of his life, turning out uninspired monuments, portrait busts, and cemetery sculptures which were much admired. He executed what has been termed "perhaps the most vacuous" of all statues of Washington. Bailly was issued a patent for a Statuette in 1863 and for a Statuette of Lincoln in 1865. He was elected an Academician by the Pennsylvania Academy of Fine Arts in 1856 and taught at that institution in 1876 and 1877. He died in Philadelphia at the age of fifty-eight.

BAKER, NATHAN F. (active 1841–47, Cincinnati), an exhibitor at the National Academy of Design, New York.

BALL, THOMAS (1819–1911) was born in Charlestown, Massachusetts. He inherited his interest in art from his father, who was a moderately successful sign painter. His father's death made it necessary for Thomas to leave school and go to work to earn a living for his mother and sisters. For a time he worked in the New England Museum, as errand boy, janitor, and handy man. While he was in the museum he became interested in the portraits displayed there and began to try to copy them. Soon he set himself up as a portrait painter and miniaturist. At the suggestion of a friend he tried his hand at modeling in clay. Much of the time while he was thus employed he was obliged to add to his income by singing. In 1848 he sang the title role of Elijah at the first performance of that oratorio in this country. In 1854, deciding to make sculpture his lifework, he went to Italy, settling in Florence. He returned to Boston to execute his equestrian Washington, now in the Public Gardens. In 1864 he returned to Florence, where he remained busy and happy until 1897 when he returned to the home of his daughter[1] in Montclair, New Jersey, where he died in 1911, aged ninety-two. Thomas Ball patented five of his works: in 1850, a bust of Jenny Lind; in 1853, a bust of Daniel Webster, and a statue of Webster; in 1857, a bust of Napoleon; in 1858, a statuette of Henry Clay. His autobiography, *My Three Score Years and Ten,* reveals him as a man of sweet-tempered charm and attractive simplicity of character.

BALLIN, J. (active 1842), an exhibitor at the National Academy of Design, New York.

BARBEE, WILLIAM R. (1820–68) was born at the family homestead near Luray, Virginia. His early attempts at carving and whittling convinced his parents and teachers that he was a good-for-nothing dreamer. At the age of fifteen he was sent to Richmond College, where he graduated with honors at eighteen. He decided then that he wanted to be a sculptor but that first he would earn money with which to go to Italy. He began to study law and was admitted to the bar at the age of twenty-one. Specializing in criminal law, he "amassed sufficient funds" in ten years to depart from Virginia for travel and study in Europe. He settled in Florence, where he came under the influence of Joel T. Hart (*q.v.*) and Hiram Powers (*q.v.*). Two of his principal works, the *Coquette* and the *Fisher Girl,* are obviously "inspired" by the works of Hart and Powers. Both of these creations were exhibited in New York in 1859, where they excited much comment and a ready sale was found for replicas at fabulous prices. One critic, writing of the *Fisher Girl,* says, "We unhesitatingly pronounce the carving of that fishing-net one of the most perfect triumphs of the chisel, in mechanical detail, that we have ever beheld . . . " When the sculptor himself returned to the United States in 1860 the ladies of Luray gave a reception in his honor, and other friends in Washington arranged for the government to offer him rent-free space in the Capitol building for a studio, in order to induce him to come there to execute a government commission. This work was abruptly terminated by the outbreak of the Civil War. The sculptor died at his home in 1868. His son Herbert also became a sculptor.

BARTHOLOMEW, EDWARD SHEFFIELD (1822–58) was born at Colchester, Connecticut. His early efforts in art were frowned upon by his father. Edward was first apprenticed to a bookbinder, and later to a dentist in Hartford. He did not do well at either trade; his father always claimed that Edward had been a clever, industrious boy until he read the life of Benvenuto Cellini, which "put the Devil in him." He tried to copy old pictures and neglected his work. The paintings by Cole, West, and Lawrence at the Wadsworth Athenaeum had "an astonishing effect upon his mind." He determined to be an artist and studied for a year in the life school of the National Academy of Design in New York, but on his return to Hartford he discovered to his dismay that he was color-blind. This

[1] Wife of the sculptor, William Couper.

turned his attention to sculpture. He received some instruction and materials from James Batterson, the proprietor of a local marbleyard. In 1848, after his appointment as curator of the Wadsworth Athenaeum, he went again to New York to attend lectures on anatomy and while there he contracted smallpox, which left him crippled and in poor health. On his return to Hartford some sympathetic friends enabled him to go to Italy to visit "the grave of Empire and the throne of Art." Arriving in Rome in 1851 he immediately set to work modeling a relief of *Blind Homer Led by His Daughter,* and busts of Washington and Sappho. He was enchanted with life in Italy and said he felt as though he had been born in Rome in 1851. He visited Athens and made a trip to Egypt shortly before his death in Naples, aged thirty-six. One of his patrons, George Read of Baltimore, was so enthusiastic about Bartholomew's sculpture that he bought copies of all his works. Another Baltimore patron, Enoch Pratt, made a practice of paying him double the price he asked for his sculpture. His sculptural works are marred by a relentless emphasis on accessories and details. Some of his principal works are: a monument to Charles Carroll, in Baltimore; *Commerce;* and *Ganymede and the Eagle of Jupiter.* A large collection of his sculpture is now in the Wadsworth Athenaeum.

BATTIN, T. (active 1842) was active in New York City in 1842 when he made a portrait bust of Philip Hone's daughter Mary. Apparently the mention of Mr. Battin in the Hone *Diaries* and his contribution to the Exhibition at the National Academy of Design are the only records of this artist.

BATCHELLOR, FREDERICK S. (active c.1850) was probably born in Providence, Rhode Island. He was trained as a marble carver in Tingley's stoneyards there. Only a few pieces of sculpture, all portrait busts, were executed by Batchellor because his main interest was in painting. In this he resembles another Rhode Island sculptor, George O. Annable, who also worked at Tingley's.

BERGER, H. (active 1865). United States Patents for Designs were issued to H. Berger for the following: a bust of Abraham Lincoln, 1865; a bust of Alexander von Humboldt, 1867; a statuette, 1870.

BILLINGS, HAMMAT (1818–74) was born in Milton Massachusetts. During his lifetime he was known principally as an illustrator, an architect, and a designer of monuments. Apparently he also tried his hand at sculpture; in 1867 he patented a statuette. Jarves says of him, "The mere overflow of his mind would make a reputation for the common run of architects and artists." He died in Boston.

BLANCHARD, ALONZO (active 1843) secured the first patent issued for a piece of sculpture under the Patent Act of 1842.

BLYTHE, DAVID G. (1815–65) was born in East Liverpool, Ohio. As a child he developed skill in drawing and woodcarving and at the age of fifteen he was apprenticed to Joseph Woodwell, a carver in Pittsburgh. In 1845 Blythe carved a figure of Lafayette in walnut which still stands before the Fayette County Courthouse in Uniontown, Pennsylvania. Few (if any) of his other sculptural works or carvings seem to have been identified and Blythe is remembered today chiefly as a painter of portraits and humorous scenes of life in Pittsburgh. He wrote many poems which were published in local newspapers under the pen-name of "Boots." Except for his apprenticeship to the woodcarver, Blythe was entirely self-taught. He worked almost entirely in western Pennsylvania, earning his living principally as an itinerant portrait painter. He died in East Liverpool in 1865 at the age of fifty.

BRACKETT, EDWARD AUGUSTUS (1818–1908) was born in Vassalboro, Maine. In 1835 he went with his parents to Cincinnati and there he took up the study of art. For the most part he was self-taught. He made portrait busts in Cincinnati and Washington and in 1841 he opened a studio in Boston. He designed and built a house outside the city and there he experimented in raising hothouse grapes and game birds. His growing interest in things of this sort gradually led him to give up sculpture, especially after he became connected with the Government Commission on Land Fisheries. He invented a fish-hatching trap which it is believed remains in use today much as he designed it. His interests embraced the writing of poetry, of which three volumes were published; he also wrote a book on spiritualism, and in his capacity as chairman of the Commission on Land Fisheries he wrote its Annual Reports for twenty-seven years. He did not go to Italy to study sculpture. Of his work in this field, other than portrait busts, his principal work was the *Shipwrecked Mother,* in Mount Auburn Cemetery. He was an admirer of Washington Allston and had the melancholy task of making Allston's death mask, from which he afterwards carved portrait busts in marble. Brackett died in Winchester, Massachusetts, aged ninety.

BROWN, HENRY KIRKE (1814–86) was born in Leyden, Massachusetts. As a youth he was skilled in the art of cutting silhouettes. In 1832 he was apprenticed to the leading portrait painter in Boston, Chester Harding. In 1836 he went west to Cincinnati to settle there as a portrait painter. While in Cincinnati he took up modeling and decided to become a sculptor. He worked as a surveyor on the railroad in order to earn enough money to take him to Italy to study. For a while he stayed in Albany, New York, making portrait busts of the local notables, and finally he was able to sail for Italy. He returned to the United States in 1846 and opened a studio in New York where he experimented in casting small bronzes. His best work is the equestrian Washington in Union Square, New York. He had great influence on a number of younger sculptors who were his pupils. He was one of the first to maintain that study in Italy was not a necessity for sculptors. He died in Newburgh, New York, aged seventy-two.

BULLET, CHARLES (active 1850–60), a French (?) sculptor who worked in Cincinnati.

BUNTING, E. V. (active 1865), Patentee—bust of Lincoln, 1865.

BUTTI, GUIDO (active 1853), an exhibitor at the National Academy of Design, New York.

CAREW, JOSEPH (active 1849) was a plasterworker and sculptor who worked in Boston.

CAREW, THOMAS (active 1860), Patentee—medallion portrait of Theodore Parker, 1860.

CARLIN, J. [JOHN?] (active 1864–67) exhibited sculpture in the annual Artist's Fund Society exhibitions in 1864 and 1867 in New York. Possibly these were the work of the miniature painter John Carlin,[2] a deaf-mute who was then working in New York.

CHRISTISENSSEN, W. (active 1865), Patentee—statues, masonic group, 1865.

CLEVENGER, SHOBAL VAIL (1812–43) was born in Middletown, Ohio. At the age of sixteen he was apprenticed to a stonecutter and later he removed to Cincinnati, where he worked in the marbleyard of David Guion for four years. His portrait bust of the editor of a local paper brought the young sculptor to the attention of Nicholas Longworth, who helped him to study anatomy at Ohio Medical College. In 1840 Longworth lent him the money with which to go to Europe. Clevenger went to Florence but remained there for only a short time as he was suddenly taken seriously ill in 1843. He died on board ship, homeward bound, in that year. Due, perhaps, to his early training in stonecutting and his study of anatomy, a few of his portrait busts are of very good quality. In view of his very brief career as an artist he is perhaps more important as the father of Dr. Shobal Vail Clevenger (1843–1920), a pioneer in reforming the treatment of the insane.

CRANE, M. H. (active 1865), Patentee—bust of Lincoln, 1865.

CRAWFORD, THOMAS[3] (1813–57) was born in New York City. At the age of fourteen he was apprenticed to a wood carver and later worked at the stoneyard of Frazee and Launitz (*q.v.*), the leading tombstone cutters in the city. He studied anatomy in the National Academy of Design. His good work interested his employers, who assisted him to go to Italy to study further. He went to Rome in 1835, carrying with him letters to Thorwaldsen, in whose studio he worked for a short time. He received a commission from the government for sculpture to decorate the Capitol in Washington but did not live to see his designs completed. In 1856 he began to suffer from a tumor of the eye which grew in malignance, ending his life the following year in severe agony. He died in London, whither he had gone for treatment. Excepting his work at the Capitol, his best-known work is the Washington monu-

[2] 1813–1891.
[3] See Chapter IV, "Clay Figures: Thomas Crawford, the Grecian Genius."

ment in Richmond, Virginia. His son, F. Marion Crawford, born in Italy in 1854, became one of the most popular and successful novelists of the 1880's and 90's.

DAY, BENJAMIN (active 1833–37), a stonecutter and sculptor active in Lowell, Massachusetts, 1833–37.

DEXTER, HENRY (1806–76) was born at Nelson, New York, on a farm in the middle of a wilderness. Henry's childish efforts at drawing and painting were taken to be evidence of inborn sinfulness. The sudden disappearance or death of his father in 1817 prompted the remaining members of the family to move to Connecticut. Here Henry was boarded out with a kindly farmer who allowed him to attend school in the winter. Later he was apprenticed to a blacksmith, with whom he remained for five years. During this period his interest in art developed, and he tried his hand at portrait painting. At the end of his apprenticeship he married a niece of the portrait painter Francis Alexander, who advised him to stick to forge and anvil if he wanted to earn a living. Dexter followed his advice for a number of years until about 1836, when he decided that in spite of everything he wanted to paint. Alexander helped him to establish himself in Boston, where he opened a studio about 1838. Through a fortunate coincidence Dexter acquired a mass of modeling clay that had been left in Boston by Horatio Greenough. This acquisition inspired in him a desire to become a sculptor, and when his first attempt was successful—a portrait bust of the Mayor of Boston—he felt he had at last found his career. From this time forward he was scarcely ever without commissions. In 1842 he patented a "sculptor's apparatus" and in 1857 patented a statue of General Warren. When Charles Dickens was in Boston he posed for Dexter, and the resulting bust pleased the author and his wife and made a tidy sum for the artist, whose agent sold casts in the different cities in which Dickens lectured. In 1857 Dexter conceived a plan to execute a gallery of portraits of all the state governors then in office and of President Buchanan. In the execution of this plan the sculptor traveled to every state of the Union and on his return to Boston exhibited thirty-one portrait busts in the State House. In a published list of works by Dexter totaling 199, only 18 are *not* portrait busts. Among these 18 are a few paintings, while chief among the sculptured figures is the once famous *Binney Child,* long the most admired monument in Mount Auburn Cemetery. Dexter, too busy with portrait commissions, never felt the urge to go to Italy. He died, lamented by many friends, in Cambridge, Massachusetts, aged seventy.

DIXEY, GEORGE, and DIXEY, JOHN V. (active c.1817–1834). Little is known of these two brothers other than the notice in Dunlap's *History of the . . . Arts of Design in the United States.* They were the sons of John Dixey, an Irish sculptor

trained in the Royal Academy, London, and in Italy, who emigrated to Philadelphia about 1789. They were both trained by their father. Dunlap lists as the work of George: *Theseus Finding His Father's Sword; St. Paul in the Island of Malta;* and *Theseus and the Wild Boar.* John V. Dixey is credited with a bas-relief of *St. John Writing the Revelations.* He also exhibited some paintings at the National Academy of Design.

DORIAN, T. H. (active 1867), Patentee—statuette, 1867.

DRUMMOND, J. B. (active 1864), Patentee—bas relief of General McClellan, 1864. Possibly this is the Scottish sculptor James Drummond, Edinburgh 1816–1877(?).

DUBOIS, MRS. CORNELIA (active in New York 1843–50). The principal notice of this sculptor is to be found in Mrs. Lee's *Familiar Sketches of Sculpture and Sculptors* (Boston, 1854). According to this source Mrs. Dubois discovered her talent for sculpture when she was called in to criticize a bust that was being modeled of her father (c.1842). Although she wished to take lessons in modeling, her fragile health allowed her only time to receive the instruction "to keep her clay moist until her work was completed." However, in spite of poor health, and with only this bit of information to guide her, we are told "she continued to mould." Among her works were *Cupid and Psyche,* a *Novice,* likenesses of her children, and a head of the Madonna, the latter finished in marble—"a laborious and exciting work, which injured her health to such a degree, that her physician interdicted her devotion to the arts." She produced over thirty cameo likenesses, and when she traveled in Italy, "where she desired the first artist in cameos to give her lessons," she was told that he could teach her nothing. After her return to New York she was compelled to give up sculpture, "delicacy of health has of late wholly interfered with these arduous though elegant employments," though she found the energy to instruct a class of young ladies in the art and generously assisted other artists on their way, among them Edward Brackett. Mrs. Lee concludes, "Whilst all who know her admire the artist for her wonderful talents, her unceasing energy, and philanthropic exertions, they too behold in her the perfect wife, mother, and friend, and the elegant and accomplished woman, presiding over the social circle. Her heart remains true to the gentlest influences of Nature, while her genius is ever responsive to immortal art." Mrs. Dubois was an active patroness of the Children's Hospital in New York.

DUNLAP, JAMES BOLIVER (1825–?) was born in Indianapolis, Indiana. He was entirely self-taught in the arts of painting, modeling, wood engraving, and drawing cartoons. For a time he worked in Indianapolis but early in his career (c.1850?) he went to California for his health. While in California he had a studio in San Francisco and executed a portrait bust of

Captain John Sutter.[4] Returning to Indianapolis, Dunlap made a bust of Abraham Lincoln during the Presidential campaign in 1860. After this point there seems to be no record of his career.

EARNSHAW, J. B. (active 1862), Patentee—design for a monument, 1862.

ELLIS, SALATHIEL (active 1842–64) was born in Toronto, Canada. He was active as a medalist in New York between 1845 and 1860, and in 1862 he patented a medallion portrait of Lincoln.

FOLEY, MARGARET E. (?–1877). According to some accounts, Margaret E. Foley was born in Dorset, Vermont, early in the nineteenth century. She was almost entirely self-taught, beginning her career as a sculptor by whittling and carving in wood. For seven years she worked in Boston, doing cameos and portrait busts. On going to Rome she became a member of the band of female sculptors led by Harriet Hosmer. Here she applied herself to the making of portrait busts and especially portrait medallions. It is reported that the painter Bierstadt said he knew of no artist who, in the same length of time, had made so many portraits as Miss Foley. The *Boston Advertiser* (January, 1878) claims, "Miss Foley's exquisite medallions and sculptures ought to be reproduced in photograph. Certainly she is a most devoted artist, and America has not had so many sculptors among women that she can afford to forget any one of them." She designed the central fountain for Horticultural Hall at the Centennial in Philadelphia in 1876. Unceasing work and the unfortunate climate of Rome combined to ruin her health and she died at Meran in the Austrian Tyrol, where she was trying to rest and recuperate.

FRANKENSTEIN, JOHN A. (1817–1881) came to the United States with his parents from Germany in 1831 when he was about sixteen years old. The family—all of them artists—settled in Ohio. John and his brothers were taught painting, and he is supposed to have taught himself the art of modeling. He studied anatomy in the Ohio Medical College and later worked as a portrait painter in Philadelphia and New York. His portrait bust of Judge McLean is in the Cincinnati Art Museum.

FREEMAN, MRS. JAMES E. (1826–?) can be considered an American sculptor only by courtesy. She was an Italian, born Augusta Latilla. Apparently she never came to the United States. Her husband, an American painter, lived for many years in Rome, where they maintained a studio. Mr. Freeman was the author of two volumes entitled *Gatherings from an Artist's Portfolio,* which give an excellent picture of the "art-

life" in Italy. Mrs. Freeman is not to be confused with Miss Florence Freeman, an American sculptor born in Boston in 1836, who worked in Rome after 1862.

GALT, ALEXANDER (1827–63) was born in Norfolk, Virginia. In his youth he carved cameo portraits and made portrait drawings. In 1848 he went to Italy to study drawing and modeling in Florence. Later he returned to the United States, bringing with him a number of his works in sculpture. At this time he traveled in the South, taking portraits and modeling busts, until 1856 when he returned to Florence with many private commissions for busts in marble and an order from the Virginia State Legislature for a statue of Jefferson for the University of Virginia. In 1860 he returned to the United States and opened a studio in Richmond, Virginia. At the beginning of the Civil War he served as a member of the staff of Governor Letcher. In the winter of 1862 he contracted smallpox and died in Richmond. Many of his works stored in a warehouse in Richmond were destroyed when the city was burned in 1863. Among his works are *The Spirit of the South,* an ideal head; *Virginia; Sappho; Columbus;* and the Jefferson statue at the University.

GARBEILLE, PHILIP (active 1848), Patentee—bust of Zachary Taylor, 1848. Worked in New Orleans.

GARLICK, THEODATUS (1805–84) was born in Middlebury, Vermont. He was an exact contemporary of that other, more famous, Vermont sculptor, Hiram Powers. He was in other respects very much like Powers in that he had little education, an inventive turn of mind, and an interest in sculpture. He was unlike Powers in that his interest in sculpture, through medical training, led him to the humanitarian art of plastic surgery rather than to the sterilities of the Statuary Business. At the age of eleven Garlick walked from his home in Vermont to western Pennsylvania, to the home of one of his brothers, where he was taught the blacksmith's trade; later he went on to Cleveland, where another brother took him in and taught him the art of stonecutting. In 1823 he decided to study medicine and toward that end started to read in the office of Dr. Ezra Gleason in Brookfield, Ohio. Later he studied with Dr. Elijah Flower for four years. During this time he supported himself by working at his trades in the morning and studying medicine in the afternoon. He saved his earnings and went for further study to the medical school of the University of Maryland, graduating in 1843. After a few months' special study in the office of a surgeon, he settled in Youngstown, Ohio where he practiced for eighteen years. At the end of this time he went to Cleveland and opened an office with another doctor. Here he gained a reputation as a skilled surgeon from his pioneer experiments in plastic surgery. He not only invented a number of special surgical instruments and appliances, but, aided by his knowledge of blacksmithing, forged and tempered them himself. Though always engaged

---

[4] Captain Sutter had the misfortune to become a large landowner in California *before* the Gold Rush of 1849. During the Gold Rush his rights as a landowner were ignored by the gold seekers. He died a broken man, trying to establish his claim to indemnification from the Government for his losses. The news of the discovery of gold on his property precipitated the Gold Rush.

in medical work, he found time for a diversity of other interests, among them sculpture. In this line he modeled wax medallions and portrait busts of his professors at the University, of Henry Clay, Andrew Jackson, and others. He also designed pathological and anatomical models that were used for teaching purposes in the local medical schools, thus following in the footsteps of that first American sculptor, William Rush (1756–1833). When the invention of photography was announced, Dr. Garlick built himself a camera. Later he became interested in the breeding of fresh-water fish and published a treatise on the subject in 1857. (Edward Brackett [q.v.] was another sculptor interested in this subject.) Garlick also wrote a biography of Ephraim Kirby. He was married three times, his first two wives being the daughters of his old teacher, Dr. Flower. He died, aged seventy-nine, from a lingering disease of the spinal nerves.

GILES, W. A. (active 1866), Patentee—bust and clock-case, 1866.

GOULD, THOMAS RIDGEWAY (1818–81) was born in Boston, the son of a prosperous man of good social standing. Financial reverses on the death of his father in 1826 forced him to go to work to support his mother. As a young man he developed an interest in art and studied drawing and modeling with his friend William Story (q.v.) in the studio of Seth Cheney. Until the Civil War Thomas Gould was quite successful in business and only amused himself with sculpture in his spare time. However, financial disaster again overtook him, whereupon he turned to sculpture as a means of earning a living. His success as a sculptor was assured by his wide circle of friends, which included most of the prominent men in Boston. He made portrait busts of Emerson and Junius Brutus Booth. In 1868 he patented a statuette of Channing and that year sailed for Italy, where he opened a studio in Florence. The following year he produced one of his principal works, *The West Wind,* which created a sensation when exhibited in America and won him orders for seven replicas. He moved to a larger studio and there produced a *Cleopatra* and an imaginary portrait statue of King Kamehameha I of the Sandwich Islands. This statue now stands before the government buildings in Honolulu. Besides his many works in sculpture, he wrote *The Tragedian; an Essay on the Histrionic Genius of Junius Brutus Booth* (1868). He died in Florence, aged seventy-three.

GREENOUGH, HORATIO (1805–52)[5] was born in Boston. He early developed an interest in art and was encouraged in the study of sculpture by Washington Allston. As a youth he was allowed to try his hand at making copies from the plaster casts in the Boston Athenaeum. He graduated from Harvard in 1824 and then set out for Italy to continue studying sculpture. His great enthusiasm for art led him to work so hard that he became ill and was forced to return home to recuperate in 1826. In 1828 he made a bust of President Adams and

was commissioned by Robert Gilmore of Baltimore to make a portrait bust of his wife. Greenough returned to Italy in 1829 to study marble carving at the quarries of Carrara, later he settled in Florence. His first important commission was ordered by his friend J. Fenimore Cooper, for whom he made the *Chanting Cherubs.* In 1832 he received a commission from the United States Government for a statue of Washington to be placed in the rotunda of the Capitol, thus Greenough became the first American sculptor to receive an important commission from the government. In 1840 he received another government commission for a large group—*The Rescue*—which now stands on the east stair of the Capitol. Greenough came to Washington in 1842 to supervise the installation of the Washington statue and returned to Italy the following year. Increasing political disturbances in Italy decided him to return to the United States to settle permanently in 1851. His essays were published in 1852 with the title *Travels, Observations, and Experiences of a Yankee Stonecutter,* under the pen name Horace Bender. That same year he was stricken with a fatal attack of "brain-fever," dying in Somerville, Massachusetts.

GREENOUGH, RICHARD SALTONSTALL (1819–1904) was born in Boston, the youngest brother of the sculptor Horatio Greenough. He was brought up in surroundings of wealth and culture. His admiration for his brother decided him to take up sculpture, and in 1837 he went to Florence to study but returned to Boston the following year because of bad health. In 1846 he returned to Italy and settled in Rome. His most famous work is the statue of Benjamin Franklin which stands before the City Hall in Boston. The unveiling of this figure was one of the most elaborate public ceremonies ever held in Boston and it marks the high point in the career of the artist. In general his works seldom equaled in quality the works of Horatio. Richard Greenough traveled extensively in Europe and made a number of trips to the United States. He was one of the first American sculptors to work and study in Paris. He died in Rome, aged eighty-five.

HALLER, G. J. (active 1865), Patentee—bust of Lincoln, 1865.

HART, JOEL TANNER (1810–77) was born in Winchester, Kentucky, the son of poor but educated parents. Though he had little schooling, he was by nature studious. He was apprenticed to a stonecutter and builder. At the age of twenty-one he met Shobal Vail Clevenger (q.v.), who was modeling a bust of Henry Clay at Lexington, Kentucky. This fortunate meeting not only turned his attention to sculpture but also brought to his notice Henry Clay, whose features he reproduced over and over again at prices which kept him in easy circumstances for the rest of his life. After discovering his talent for modeling portrait busts, he went to the Hermitage, where Andrew Jackson posed for him. Returning to Lexington, he acquired

[5] See Chapter IV: "Clay Figures—Horatio Greenough, the Honest Yankee Stonecutter."

a great local reputation which encouraged him to travel to New York, Philadelphia, Baltimore, Washington and Richmond, taking commissions for busts and studying the statuary displayed in these centers. In 1846 the Ladies Clay Association of Richmond commissioned him to do a life-size statue of Henry Clay for the sum of $5,000. He set to work by having a series of daguerreotypes made of Mr. Clay from all angles; he took casts of his face and hands and made a complete series of measurements of the famous gentleman's anatomy and also made a study of his clothing. Relying heavily on these mechanical facts, he worked for three years creating a plaster model which he shipped to Italy in 1849. Hart set out for Florence and arrived before the cast was delivered. Settling down to wait, he spent some time traveling and studied anatomy in London for almost a year. On his way back to Florence he visited Paris and saw the Louvre. When he finally got to Florence again he found that his cast had been lost in a shipwreck, whereupon he sent to Richmond for a duplicate, which did not arrive for another year. While recovering from cholera and typhoid fever, he invented a pointing machine (patented in England and France), which was so complicated that no other sculptor would attempt to use it. Hart was naturally very enthusiastic about his invention and claimed "Thus the sculptor can produce his models in America or elsewhere, and send them to be wrought out where labor and material are cheaper, without the necessity of laboring upon them himself; the measures or points being exact ... the workman ... can produce two (portrait busts) in the time required for one in the old way."[*] He said, "Powers and the rest of them hate it like the devil." He charged one hundred guineas apiece for busts made with this machine and is said to have had ten commissions while showing it in London. His statue of Henry Clay was finally finished in 1859—thirteen years after the commission was given! He came to the United States for the unveiling of the statue and basked in glory and praise. Though he planned to open a studio in New York, the receipt of commissions for two replicas of the Clay statue from the cities of Louisville and New Orleans at $10,000 each decided him to return to Italy. Here he settled down in Florence to work at a leisurely pace, spending much time on a group called *Woman Triumphant,* which occupied him for thirty years. He seemed unable or unwilling to complete this work and is said to have refused an offer of $20,000 for it. He dreamed away the rest of his life, playing at sculpture, writing verses, and selling busts of Henry Clay whenever he needed money to prolong the comfortable and innocent idyl of his life in Florence. He died in Florence and was first buried there. His many admirers in his native state by special enactment had his body disinterred and reburied with great ceremony at the State Cemetery in Frankfort, Kentucky, in 1885. This event was responsible for the publication of several extraordinary memorials which proclaim him an immortal genius.

[*] J. J. Jarves, *Art Hints* (1855).

HAWKINS, BENJAMIN WATERHOUSE (1807–89) was born in London. He was well educated in scientific schools and made a particular study of zoology; in 1853 he made a reputation by modeling full scale a number of paleozoological specimens for the Crystal Palace at Sydenham. He came to the United States in 1868 to lecture on extinct fossil animals and was employed at the old Central Park Museum (now the American Museum of Natural History), where he executed a series of models of extinct animals for their exhibition. He was the author of a number of scientific works and wrote especially on the artistic anatomy of the horse and other animals. He died in 1889.

HAYNES, C. Y. (active 1850), Patentee—bas relief of Henry Clay, 1850. Philadelphia.

HEMENWAY, CHARLES (?–1887) was probably born in Providence, Rhode Island, early in the nineteenth century. He was trained in marble carving at Tingley's stoneyard in Providence. He executed a number of busts, among them portraits of Bishop Clark and Chief Justice Bradley. His monument to the Sprague children was long an attraction in the Swan Point Cemetery. Throughout his career he was a happy-go-lucky Bohemian, improvident and carefree; he became, at the end of his life, the object of charity and an inmate of the Dexter Asylum, where he died in 1887.

HOPPIN, THOMAS FREDERICK (1816–?) was probably born in Providence, Rhode Island. He showed artistic talent at an early age and studied art in Philadelphia and under Delaroche in Paris. In 1837 he settled in New York, where he designed some stained glass for Trinity Church. He was noted as a wood engraver and painter and also executed several pieces of sculpture. He was working in Providence in 1844.

HOSMER, HARRIET GOODHUE (1830–1908) was born in Watertown, Massachusetts, the daughter of a doctor. Her mother's death from tuberculosis decided the doctor to give Harriet an out-of-door education and unusual freedom for a little girl at that time. She grew up a tomboy, strong, tough, the terror of the neighborhood, unrestrained and willful. At the age of sixteen she was sent to Lenox, Massachusetts, to be educated by Mrs. Sedgwick, who somewhat tamed the savage and prepared her to make decorous entrances to drawingrooms. Here she became the pet of the circle of notables who came to Lenox, here she met Emerson and Fanny Kemble. She had since childhood shown a talent for modeling and after three years at Lenox decided to become a sculptor—an extraordinary and characteristically unorthodox career for a woman. For a while she studied drawing and modeling in Boston but on trying to get into a medical school to study anatomy found herself barred. Finally she was accepted at the University medical school in St. Louis, Missouri. In 1852 she went to Rome to study in the studio of John Gibson. At first Roman society was outraged by her unconventional behavior, but she went serenely on her way and soon won an enviable number of affluent friends with imposing titles. She was not only the leading female sculptor in Rome but one of the few who gained financial independence by her work. Almost every royal visitor to Rome went to her studio to come away a captive to her piquant manner, leaving behind them a jeweled bauble or at least a commission. When the Prince of Wales purchased her *Puck,* she soon sold thirty copies at one thousand dollars a piece. At one time she had enough orders to keep at least twenty Italian marble workers busy in her studio. The Empress Frederick was heard to remark that Miss Hosmer "had a genius for toes." The Queen of Naples posed for a full-length statue. The state of Missouri commissioned her for a monument to Senator Benton. Miss Hosmer spent her summers with her titled friends in England, "combining business with pleasure." Toward the end of her career she became engrossed in the study of perpetual motion and tried to invent a perpetual motion machine run by magnets. She also patented a "marble-working process" which she claimed made it possible to make marble out of common limestone. Returning to the United States, she lectured on art in the West. She died in Watertown, Massachusetts, aged seventy-eight.

HUGHES, ROBERT BALL (1806–68) was born in London. He was apprenticed to the sculptor Edward Bailey and studied in the Royal Academy school, which awarded him several prizes. He emigrated to New York about 1828/29 and a few years later settled in Dorchester, Massachusetts. Though his Royal Academy training weighed heavily in his favor and at first brought him a number of commissions, bad luck and bad judgement seemed to ruin his every work. His statue of Alexander Hamilton was destroyed by fire soon after it was unveiled, his statue of Nathaniel Bowditch at Mount Auburn was recast, and many of his portrait miniatures in wax have disappeared. After the destruction of the Canova Washington in Raleigh he was given the commission to restore the fragments, but from all accounts he was unfaithful to his contract and, it seems, he took payment of $2,500 for work he did not perform. One of his patrons in New York, John Watts DePeyster, wrote in a private letter that he considered him an eminent sculptor, but that he was an irresponsible vagabond like all artists and had stolen portraits of DePeyster's ancestors. Hughes was awarded an important commission to execute a Washington monument for Philadelphia, but the failure of the Bank of the United States in 1841 ended the project. Hughes died in Dorchester, his early promise unfulfilled.

HUNT, WILLIAM MORRIS (1824–1879) was born in Brattleboro, Vermont. Noted as a painter, he first planned to be a sculptor. His only important sculpture, a study of horses, was used in designing a mural, *Flight of Night,* at Albany.

IVES, CHAUNCEY BRADLEY (1810–94) was born at Hamden, Connecticut, near New Haven. At the age of sixteen he was apprenticed to R. F. Northrup, a woodcarver in New Haven. It is supposed that he also worked with the better-known

woodcarver and sculptor, Hezekiah Augur (1791–1858). Ives determined to become a sculptor and went to study in Boston, where he carved a bust in stone which brought him some attention. His health failing, he was ordered to a warm climate, whereupon he sailed for Italy in 1844. He settled in Florence, remaining there for seven years, then moving to Rome. On frequent trips to the United States he was successful at finding purchasers for replicas of his small marble groups to be used as parlor ornaments. Among these were: *Rebecca at the Well, Sans Souci, White Captives, Shepherd-Boy.* He executed the statue of Trumbull which stands before the State House in Hartford, Connecticut, besides a number of portrait busts.

IVES, J. J. (active 1850), an exhibitor at the National Academy of Design, New York.

JACKSON, JOHN ADAMS (1825–79) was born at Bath, Maine. At an early age he was given some training in mechanical drawing by D. C. Johnston of Boston. For a time he drew crayon portraits while apprenticed as a clerk to a Boston merchant. While still quite young he managed to get to Paris, where he studied anatomy in the life school of Charles Suisse. In 1851 he modeled a portrait of Daniel Webster and in 1853 he was in Florence making portrait busts. He returned to Paris in the following year and there he continued to turn out busts of prominent men, among them, Dr. Lyman Beecher, Wendell Phillips, and George S. Hillard. In 1858 he opened a studio in New York and in 1860 he was commissioned to execute a monument to Kane the polar explorer. Though he went to Florence to work on this monument, the commission was not carried out. From this time forward he remained in Florence, where he executed over a hundred portrait busts in addition to ideal figures and groups. Of these latter, his most important was *Eve and the Dead Abel,* a work so realistic that an English surgeon wrote an essay on the anatomy, physiology, and pathology of Abel. An ecstatic review in the Boston *Transcript,* reporting on the exhibition of the statue in that city, says, "The form of Abel is very bold ... It is dead beyond hope of any recovery; and yet, through the magic of the sculptor's art, it excites only tender and pleasing emotions." Several of his works were repeated over and over so great was the demand, notably an ideal bust called *Dawn,* and a medallion *Morning-Glory,* of which fourteen replicas were sold. He visited New York in 1867 and for the Croton Water Board did a group for the south gatehouse of the Central Park Reservoir. He died in Praccia, Italy.

JONES, ANTHONY W. (active 1818–68). A modeler of portrait busts who worked in New York.

JONES, THOMAS D. (1811–91). Tom Jones was born near Granville, Ohio. He had no education except what his own original mind absorbed. He worked as a stonecutter and mason in Ohio. In 1841 he settled in Cincinnati and worked as a marble carver and with no instruction started to carve portrait busts in wood and stone. In 1842 he set himself up as a sculptor. For fifteen years he had a studio in Cincinnati, where he became a colorful, if eccentric, member of the art group. He was an independent character, who, scorning convention, appeared on the streets in the costume of a romantic brigand, his long hair flowing from under a large hat with an upswept brim, a cloak wrapped about him like a toga. He worked in Columbus, Ohio, Nashville, Detroit, New York, and Boston. His principal work is the Lincoln monument in Columbus. He made portraits of the leading men of the day: Henry Clay, William Henry Harrison, Salmon P. Chase, and in 1865 he patented a bust of Abraham Lincoln. He died in Cincinnati. Jones wrote an account of the making of his bust of Lincoln and reports that Lincoln, on being told that he would not have to endure the discomforts of having a mask cast from his features, said: "I like your mode; when Mr. Volk of Chicago, made a bust of me, he took a plaster cast of my face, a process that was anything but agreeable."

KING, JOHN CROOKSHANKS (1806–82) was born in Ayrshire, Scotland. At the age of five he determined to become a painter. In his youth he was apprenticed to a machinist (his father's trade). In 1829 he came to the United States with his brother, entering the country at New Orleans. He worked in Louisville and Cincinnati as a machinist. In Cincinnati he met Hiram Powers and at his suggestion tried his hand at modeling. Powers praised his first efforts so highly that King decided to continue as a sculptor. He "took" portraits in the towns along the Ohio and Mississippi rivers and in 1836 was working in New Orleans. He embarked in 1840 for Boston, where he opened a studio and remained for the rest of his life. Among the portrait busts he executed in Boston are those of Emerson, John Quincy Adams, Agassiz, and Daniel Webster; of the last four replicas were sold. Much of his work was destroyed when his studio burned in 1852.

KNEELAND, HORACE (active 1830–60) exhibited portrait busts in the Annual Exhibitions of the National Academy of Design, New York.

KORNEMAN and JUNGBLUTH (active 1869), Patentees—statuette, 1869.

KUNTZE, EDWARD J. (1826–70) was born in Prussia. He came to the United States in 1844. In 1864 he patented a statuette of Schiller and in 1865 he patented statuettes of Shakespeare and Lincoln. He was elected an Associate of the National Academy of Design in 1869. He executed many portrait busts and among his ideal figures are *Psyche, Mirth, Merlin,* and *Vivien*. He died in New York.

LANDER, LOUISA (1826–?) was born in Salem, Massachusetts. Little of her early career has been recorded, but she was active in Washington in 1853 and went to Rome in 1855, where she studied under Thomas Crawford. In 1858 she was commis-sioned to make a bust of Governor Gore for the Library at Harvard. Among her other works are a portrait bust of Nathaniel Hawthorne, a reclining figure of Evangeline, and a lifesize statue of Virginia Dare. In 1860 a critic says, "Her art, and the proper study of it, called her forth to wander among strangers, in a strange land ..." In 1913 she was listed in *Who's Who* as a resident of Washington, D. C.

LAUNITZ, ROBERT EBERHARDT SCHMIDT VON DER (1806–70) was born in Riga of a good family. He was well educated in the classics and in military science. He decided, however, to become a sculptor and went to Rome to study in the studio of his uncle. Later he worked for four years in the studio of Thorwaldsen. In 1830 he arrived in New York and found employment in John Frazee's marble yard. Frazee and Launitz soon formed a partnership, and Launitz took charge of the studios. Here his knowledge of foreign languages enabled him to employ immigrant stonecutters, and his excellent training as a sculptor was an invaluable addition to the resources of the firm. The sculptor Thomas Crawford (*q.v.*) received his early training under Launitz. The portrait statue of Charlotte Canda in Greenwood Cemetery first brought Launitz some attention (1845). He published a book of tombstone designs which were, of course, immediately copied by stonecutters whose skill was not as great as his. In 1848 he was commissioned by the Kentucky Legislature for a monument to be placed in the State Cemetery at Frankfort, and in 1854 he executed a monument to Pulaski now in Savannah. Launitz was more of an artist than he was a business man and lost money on his work. At the end of the Civil War the sale of patented cast-iron statues and ready-made memorials greatly reduced his business. He died in New York.

LECONTE, A. (active 1865), Patentee—medallion of Lincoln, 1865.

LIVINGSTONE, M. L. (active 1860), Patentee—medallion of Washington Irving, 1860.

MACDONALD, JAMES WILSON ALEXANDER (1824–1908) was born in Steubenville, Ohio. He showed artistic talent at an early age, and on seeing a bust of Washington decided to become a sculptor. His father wanted to apprentice him to a blacksmith, so, at the age of sixteen, he ran away from home. He made his way to St. Louis, where he found employment in a publishing house. He made rapid headway in the firm for which he worked and in eleven years was a senior partner, meanwhile carrying on his study of art at night in the studio of a local painter. In 1849 he went to New York to continue his studies. Sometime thereafter he retired from the St. Louis firm and settled in New York to devote all his time to art. He executed a number of Civil War monuments and many portrait busts and medallions. Some of his time was spent in lecturing on anatomy and in writing art criticism. He owned what was then reputed to be the original plaster bust of Washington by Houdon, from which he made many casts for sale. He died in Yonkers.

MACHEN, W. H. (active 1865), Patentee—monument to the memory of Abraham Lincoln, 1865.

MANLEY, F. (active mid 19th century), made portrait busts in New York.

MARSHALL, W. M. (active 1868), Patentee—medallion of General Grant, 1868.

McKAYE, H. E., and S. J. McKAYE (active 1867), Patentees —three statuettes, 1867.

McLAUGHLIN, J. W. (active 1865), Patentee—monument, 1865.

MILLER, R. (active 1866), Patentee—cemetery monument, 1866.

MILLS, CLARK (1810–83) was born in Onondaga County, New York. He had a very hard youth as a common laborer, knocking about the country, drifting from one job to another. He made his way to New Orleans and about 1830 settled in Charleston, South Carolina, where he worked as a plaster molder. About 1835 he attempted his first works in sculpture —modeling busts in clay. He was clever with his hands and had an inventive turn of mind. He is credited with inventing about this time a new process for making life masks. He made many portraits and studied marble carving. His bust of Calhoun was purchased by the city of Charleston in 1846, and the sculptor was presented with an honorary gold medal by Calhoun's admirers in Charleston. He was befriended by J. S. Preston, who had been a patron of Hiram Powers and through him Mills received a number of portrait commissions. Mills was about to set out for Italy when Preston suggested that he should see the sculpture in Washington first. On his way to Washington, Mills stopped in Richmond to see the Houdon statue of Washington—it was the first statue he had ever seen. While in Washington he was awarded the commission to make an equestrian statue of Jackson. This monument, dedicated in 1853, was a sensational success. Although it has been called a "prodigious Congressional joke on art" it is also a monument to the daring and persistent ingenuity of its creator. It is to be doubted that Mills had ever seen an equestrian monument, he had to design and build his own foundry and train his assistants; in this respect the Jackson monument is an extraordinary achievement. Unhampered by traditional fears, Mills successfully balanced the horse on its hind feet— a spectacular bit of mechanical trickery which immediately won for him the highest praise as an artist and a fifty-thousand-dollar commission from Congress for an equestrian Washington. In 1860 Thomas Crawford's *Armed Freedom,* now surmounting the dome of the Capitol, was cast by Mills. New Orleans and Nashville commissioned replicas of his

Jackson Monument. He also executed many portrait busts and at the end of his career was planning a colossal Lincoln monument composed of over thirty large figures. In 1854 he patented his bust of Calhoun and in 1855 he patented his designs for equestrian statues. His son, Theodore Augustus Mills (1839–1916), was also a sculptor. Clark Mills died in Washington, aged seventy-three.

MILLS, F. (active 1865), Patentee—bust of Lincoln, 1865.

MORGAN, D. (active 1866–68), Patentee—bust of Lincoln, 1866; Soldiers monument, 1867; bust of F. Douglas, 1868.

MORRISON, M. (active 1838), an exhibitor at the National Academy of Design, New York.

MORTIMER, GEORGE D. (active c.1838–1842), a sculptor active in New York who exhibited at the Apollo Gallery and the National Academy of Design.

MOZIER, JOSEPH (1812–70) was born in Burlington, Vermont. He spent his early manhood in Ohio and is known to have been in 1840 successfully engaged in business in New York. About 1845 he retired from business to give his whole attention to studying sculpture in Florence, Italy. Later he established a studio in Rome. He is one of the few sculptors of the time who did *not* make a great number of portrait busts, his financial success in business having relieved him of earning a living in this way. Most of his works are "ideal" figures inspired by contemporary American literature, the Bible, and classical mythology. During his lifetime his works were very popular, his *Wept of Wish-Ton-Wish* (a heroine in one of Cooper's novels) was considered his best work. His *Undine* won the grand prize at an exhibition in Rome in 1867. He died while traveling in Switzerland, at Faido.

MULLER, CHARLES (active 1856–68), Patentee—statuette, Burton as Captain Cuttle, 1856; four figures, 1868; figure and base, 1868.

OLIVER, L. (active 1859), an exhibitor at the National Academy of Design, New York.

PALMER, ERASTUS DOW[7] (1817–1904) was born in Pompey, Onondaga County, New York. He early showed mechanical skill and became while still quite young an expert carpenter and builder. As a pastime he took up the art of making cameo portraits and from this he turned to sculpture in a larger form when the strain upon his eyes became too great. The strong religious cast of many of his works attracted the attention of the clergy, and a number of his sculptures were exhibited in New York in 1856 as "The Palmer Marbles" in the hall of the Church of the Divine Unity, 548 Broadway. He maintained a studio for many years in Albany and there did many portraits of local men and women, cemetery monuments and ideal figures. He did not go to Italy to study though he made a trip to Europe in 1874. His statue of Robert Livingston won a medal at the Centennial in Philadelphia in 1876. His son Walter was for many years a well-known landscape painter in New York. Erastus Dow Palmer died in Albany. Many of his works are now in the Albany Institute of History and Art.

PARKER, LIFE (active 1837), a carver and sculptor employed by Major Benjamin Day in Lowell, Massachusetts, 1837.

PHILIP, W. H. H. (active 1865), Patentee—bust of Lincoln, 1865.

PIATTI, ANTHONY (active 1850–57), an exhibitor at the National Academy of Design, New York.

PLASSMAN, ERNST (1823–77) was born in Westphalia. He went to New York in 1853 and remained there for the rest of his life. He was the proprietor of an art school and the organizer of the Society of Art, an association of German artists and art-lovers in New York. He executed a number of statues, notably those of Franklin, in Printing House Square, New York; the Vanderbilt statue in the Freight Depots on Hudson Square; Tammany in Tammany Hall.

POWELL, J. (active 1865–66), Patentee—medallion of Lincoln, 1865; medallion of Grant, 1866.

POWERS, HIRAM[8] (1805–73) was born in Woodstock, Vermont. He went west with his parents and lived near Cincinnati, Ohio. About 1829 he took up modeling in clay and wax. From 1829 to 1834 he worked in Dorfeuille's Western Museum in Cincinnati, making wax figures and automata. In 1835 he began his career as a sculptor, setting out for Washington on his way to Italy. He modeled several busts in Washington, among them a portrait of Andrew Jackson, a work he never surpassed in later years. He arrived in Florence in 1837. His most famous work was his *Greek Slave* which was exhibited in London in 1845 and again at the Crystal Palace in 1851, where it was received with unusual enthusiasm. Powers executed many portrait busts, a few statues, and ideal figures, for which he was very well paid. He died in Florence.

PURDY, H. P. W. (active 1865), Patentee—composition in alto relievo, 1865.

RANDOLPH, JAMES THOMPSON (1817–74), a woodcarver and stonecutter, was born in Bound Brook, New Jersey. Most of his artistic life was spent in Baltimore, where he executed the McDonogh Monument, dedicated in Greenmount Cemetery in 1865.

READ, THOMAS BUCHANAN (1822–72) was born at a place called Corner Ketch, near Guthriesville in Chester County, Pennsylvania. Though his fame as a poet and painter of portraits completely overshadowed his work as a sculptor, he was in his youth employed by Shobal Vail Clevenger (*q.v.*)

as a stonecutter in Cincinnati. Principal among his sculptural works is a portrait bust of General Sheridan. His best-remembered poem is "Sheridan's Ride," a subject which also inspired one of his paintings. For a time Read was a member of the colony of American artists in Rome; he traveled in Europe and died in New York on his return to the United States.

RICHARDS, DAVID (1829–97) was born in Abergnynolwyn, Wales. He arrived in the United States some time after 1847 and worked in Utica, New York, as a stonecutter. As a sculptor he was largely self-taught. He worked in New York City and Chicago, and spent two years in Rome. His principal work is *The Confederate Soldier,* in Savannah, Georgia. He died at Woodside, Long Island.

RIMMER, WILLIAM[9] (1816–79) was born in Liverpool, England. He was brought to Nova Scotia by his parents in 1819 and later settled with them in Boston. Here William began to show his artistic talent by drawing, painting, and modeling. As a young man he engaged in various occupations—typesetting, soap-making, teaching music, and sign painting. After his marriage he became a cobbler in Brockton, Massachusetts, and there he began the study of medicine. He began in 1855 to carve in granite. In 1861 he taught anatomy at the Lowell Institute in Boston. In 1864 he published a book, *The Elements of Design.* From 1866 to 1870 he was director of the School of Design for Women at Cooper Union in New York. In 1877 he published his *Art Anatomy.* His lectures on anatomy were very popular, and a great many students came under his influence, notable among them are John LaFarge and Daniel Chester French. Only about six of his sculptures survive—*The Falling Gladiator, The Fighting Lions, The Dying Centaur, Head of St. Stephen, Alexander Hamilton, Portrait of a Woman,* and a plaster figure *Despair.* He died in South Milton, Massachusetts.

RINEHART, WILLIAM HENRY (1825–74) was born at Union Bridge, Maryland, the son of a prosperous Pennsylvania-German farmer. As a youth he did not do well at school or at farm work. Much to the disgust of his father, William displayed a talent for drawing and modeling. Finally he was apprenticed to a local stonecutter, from whose quarry he went to work in the marble yard of the Baltimore firm of Sisson. In Baltimore he began his art studies in the night classes of the Maryland Institute of Mechanic Arts. After attracting some local attention by his work he was enabled to go to Italy to study in 1855. In 1858, after a short visit in Baltimore, he went back to Italy to settle permanently in Rome, where he died at the age of forty-nine. He left his estate in trust for "the promotion of a more highly cultivated taste for art among the people of my native state and of assisting young men in the study of the Art of Sculpture . . ." The income from his estate has been used, as he requested, to send young

---

[7] See Chapter IV: "Clay Figures—Erastus Dow Palmer, the Inspired Carpenter."
[8] See Chapter IV: "Clay Figures—Hiram Powers, the Sublime Mechanic."

[9] See Chapter IV: "Clay Figures—William Rimmer, Artist, Physician, Eccentric."

Americans to Rome to study sculpture. In addition to the scholarships which keep Rinehart's memory green, Baltimore has honored him by naming an art school, a public school, and galleries in her cultural institutions after him.

ROGERS, JOHN (1829–1904) was born in Salem, Massachusetts. He was well educated, but failing eyesight forced him to give up the study of engineering. He worked for eight years as a machinist, having charge of the railroad repair shops at Hannibal, Missouri. As a pastime he started modeling in clay. He went to Europe in 1858 and worked for a short time in Rome in the studio of Spence (an English sculptor), but soon returned to the United States. His early group *The Slave Auction* was given much publicity by Abolitionist orators. By the end of the Civil War Rogers' Groups had become very popular—they were long considered the ideal wedding gift. They were appealing in subject, they were widely advertised, and moderate in cost. It is estimated that one hundred thousand plaster copies were sold during the sculptor's lifetime. President Lincoln's family said that the portrait statuette of Lincoln in the group *Council of War* was the best likeness of the President ever made. In addition to selling thousands of his patented groups, Rogers made a good thing of selling pedestals, garden urns, and "refinishing color" to be applied to his plaster groups during spring house-cleaning. He exhibited twenty-nine groups at the Centennial in Philadelphia in 1876 which won a commendation "for excellence in the fine art of sculpture." Between 1862 and 1870 twenty-two design patents were issued to him. He was the first sculptor to make a success in selling sculpture by mail order. His importance is principally that of a recorder of the American scene of his time, and it is as a reporter that he carved for himself a special niche in American art history. He died at his home in New Canaan, Connecticut.

ROGERS, RANDOLPH (1825–92) was born in Waterloo, New York, while his parents were moving west to settle in Ann Arbor, Michigan. In his youth he worked at various jobs and had some success in selling his drawings. He came to New York and attracted the favorable attention of his employers (dry-goods merchants) by modeling their portraits. They lent him funds with which to study in Italy, whither he went in 1848, to Florence. In 1851 he settled permanently in Rome. On the death of Thomas Crawford in 1857 he was given the task of completing some of the work Crawford had been commissioned to do for the National Capitol. Rogers made frequent trips to the United States and was very successful in getting public and private commissions. He was a very important figure in the Roman art colony and was elected a Councilor of the Academy of St. Luke. His *Ruth* and *Nydia* were among the most popular attractions of the Centennial in Philadelphia in 1876. He made many replicas of these which are to be found in the collections of our older art museums. A visitor to his studio reports, "He had lately made a statue

of Nydia, the blind girl of Pompeii, which had a great popular success, particularly among Americans, who ordered many replicas for their houses . . . I once went to his studio and saw seven Nydias, all in a row, all listening, all groping, and seven marble cutters at work, cutting them out. It was a gruesome sight."[20] He died in Rome, leaving all his casts to the Art Gallery of the University of Michigan.

SEAGER (active 1834), active in Salem, Massachusetts, in 1834 making bronze portrait medallions.

SIBBELL, JOSEPH (d. 1907), a German woodcarver active in Cincinnati in the mid 19th century. He made the statue of St. Patrick, now in St. Patrick's Cathedral, New York, and died in New York.

SIMMONS, FRANKLIN (1839–1913). Though Franklin Simmons does not from the chronological point of view belong to the group of sculptors treated here, he is included as a specimen of the later generation which followed closely in the footsteps of his predecessors. He was born in Webster, Maine, and early showed an interest in art. After working at various jobs he went to Boston, where he studied in the studio of John Adams Jackson (*q.v.*). Later he opened a studio of his own in Lewiston, Maine. He became an itinerant artist, traveling through Maine painting and modeling portraits. In Brunswick he remained to do portraits of the faculty of Bowdoin College, later moving on to Portland, where he executed many portrait commissions. About 1859 he received his first commission for a large monument, that of General Hiram G. Berry at Rockland. In 1866 he was in Washington, making portrait busts and patented medallions of the military and political figures there. In 1867 he went to Rome, where he remained for the rest of his life, almost untouched by the great changes which took place in the art world in the last half of the century. He bequeathed his estate to the Portland (Maine) Art Association.

STARKEY, E. J. (active 1865), Patentee—statuette, 1865.

STEBBINS, EMMA (1815–82) was born in New York. She was brought up in comfortable surroundings and her early efforts at drawing and painting were encouraged by her family and friends. At the age of forty-two she decided to become a sculptor "throwing aside her palette." Doubtless she was prompted in this move by the success of Harriet Hosmer. In 1857 she proceeded to Rome to study with Paul Akers. Here she became a member of the little band of female sculptors centering around the actress Charlotte Cushman. Among Miss Stebbins's principal works are *The Angel of the Waters,* a fountain in Central Park, New York; a statue of Columbus, also in New York; and a statue of Horace Mann, in Boston. For many years Miss Stebbins lived as the companion of Miss Cushman, with whom she returned to the United States in

[20] D. M. Armstrong, *Day before Yesterday* (1920).

1870. Miss Stebbins wrote a memoir of her friend and edited her letters, publishing them in 1877. Miss Stebbins also wrote occasional poems. She died in New York.

STEPHENSON, PETER (1823–?) was born in Yorkshire, England. In 1827 he was brought to the United States, where his father settled on a farm in Wayne County, New York. As a child he drew and painted and was an expert whittler. In 1834 the family moved to Michigan, where his father died. Some time later Peter was apprenticed to a watchmaker in Buffalo, New York, and here he made some cameo portraits. In 1840 he carved a portrait bust—the first he had ever seen. In 1843 he set out for Boston to become a sculptor. Although he arrived in "the Athens of America" penniless, friendless, and in poor health, he earned enough money as a sculptor to sail in 1845 for Rome, where he remained for almost two years. Returning to Boston, he carved in Vermont marble a statue of *The Wounded Indian,* which was exhibited in the Crystal Palace in 1851. In 1853 he wrote an autobiographical note which states, "It is now about twelve years since I first considered myself an artist; and for the benefit of those who come after me, and think themselves much neglected because they do not receive orders for ideal works, I will state that I last week (January 1853) received the first order for an ideal work, and that, too, at a price that would discourage a stone-cutter.

"I do not, however, complain; the way to make up for hard luck is to work the more industriously. I have never received a lesson from any one, nor a cent of money that the sweat of my brow did not earn.

"I have cut between six and seven hundred cameo likenesses, about two thousand fancy designs, and several busts and statues."

Stephenson opened a studio and exhibition room in Amory Hall in Boston. In 1852 he patented three medallion portraits

STONE, HORATIO (c. 1808–1875) was born in Jackson, New York, the son of a farmer. His early attempts at whittling and carving were considered by his parents as time-wasting sinfulness, and as a result of this lack of appreciation Horatio ran away from home. He managed to get along somehow, studied medicine and for a while practiced in New York. In 1848 he suddenly abandoned medicine for sculpture, settling in Washington. Here he executed portrait busts of prominent political figures. In 1859 he was the prime mover in organizing the Washington Union Art Association, of which he was president. The purpose of this organization was to get the government to appoint a commission of American artists to supervise the decoration of the Capitol—work which was then being carried on under the sole direction of Captain Meigs, an engineer. Although the commission was appointed in 1859, Captain Meigs's personal lobby had it abolished within a year. Almost the only result of the commission was a report criticizing the spending of public funds on second-rate (and

worse) decorations, contracted for by the yard and painted by foreign journeymen. Henry Kirke Brown, the sculptor, (*q.v.*) and Lambdin and Kensett, two painters, were the members of the unfortunate commission. An article in *The Century,* commenting on the formation of the association, says, "Art is sadly caricatured at Washington. Commissions are obtained there, as they get water at Paris, by boring; by private or personal or political favor."

Horatio Stone went to Italy on two occasions to study sculpture. His bust of Taney won him a medal from the Maryland Institute of Mechanic Arts in 1857. At the time of his death the *Art Journal* reports, "Had he given his attention earlier to the study of art, under a competent master, he might have achieved lasting fame." A poem "Freedom" was published by Stone in Washington in 1864.

STORY, WILLIAM WETMORE[11] (1819–95) was born in Salem in 1819, the son of Joseph Story a lawyer and later a United States Supreme Court Justice. He was educated at Harvard and after his graduation from the Harvard Law School in 1840 decided to become a sculptor. In 1856 he settled in Rome, where he remained for the rest of his life. When his statue of Cleopatra became the sensation of the London Exposition of 1862, his reputation as an artist was made. He was an important member of the Roman art colony, the friend of many noted men and women, and the author of several volumes of poetry, legal treatises, biography, art criticism, etc. His career has been recorded fully in Henry James's book *William Wetmore Story and His Friends.* He died in Vallombrosa.

THOM, JAMES (1802–50) was born near Lochlee in Scotland. As a youth he was apprenticed to a builder at Kilmarnock. and here he developed a skill at ornamental stone carving. One of his first works was a bust of Robert Burns. Most of his works were inspired by Burns's poems—his most successful work was the *Tam o' Shanter* group originally carved direct in the stone without any preliminary sketch. When this group was sent on tour in England in 1829 it was extremely popular and sixteen replicas were ordered. Another popular subject was *Old Mortality,* a copy of which is now in Laurel Hill Cemetery, in Philadelphia. Thousands of copies of the Tam o' Shanter group were made and sold by agents.[12] The absconding of one of these agents to America with Thom's profits brought him to this country in pursuit about 1836. He was able to recover some of his money and decided to settle in Newark, New Jersey. Here he continued to make replicas of his famous groups, statues of Robert Burns, and garden ornaments. While looking for a suitable stone for sculpture, he is said to have discovered the valuable freestone

[11] See Chapter IV: "Clay Figures—William Wetmore Story, the Boston Lawyer in Rome."
[12] A replica of the *Tam o'Shanter* group may be seen in Fairmount Park, Philadelphia.

quarries at Little Falls, New York. The ornamental stonework on Trinity Church was executed by him. Later he settled on a farm near Ramapo and apparently gave up sculpture as a profession. He died in New York.

TRAUGH, S. A. (active 1865), Patentee—bust of Lincoln, 1865.

VOLK, LEONARD WELLS (1828–95) was born in Wellstown, New York, the son of a stonecutter in whose shop he began to learn the trade at the age of sixteen. For a time he was an itinerant workman, carving tombstones in various parts of Massachusetts and New York. In 1848 he settled in St. Louis, Missouri, where he began the study of art with a view to becoming a sculptor, meanwhile supporting himself as a stonecutter. One of his first works in marble was a copy of Joel Hart's bust of Henry Clay. In 1855, with money lent him by his relative Stephen A. Douglas, Volk went to Rome, where he remained for almost two years. On his return to the United States in 1857 he settled in Chicago. Here he became a leader in the art activities of the city. He was the founder of the Chicago Academy of Design in 1867 and its president for a number of years. His fame rests principally on his portrait busts of Abraham Lincoln and Stephen A. Douglas, both of which were patented in 1860. Mr. Volk published an interesting account of the making of the Lincoln portrait. He was the father of the painter Douglas Volk.

WALCUTT, WILLIAM (1819–95) was born in Columbus, Ohio. As a youth he began to paint portraits, but on seeing a piece of statuary he decided to become a sculptor. He was educated at Granville College, where he studied engineering and surveying. He studied art for four years in New York, Columbus, Ohio, and Washington. In 1852 he went abroad to London and Paris, where he studied for two years in the Yvon life school and at the Imperial School of Sculpture, which awarded him a medal for his work. He returned to New York in 1855 and opened a studio. His most notable work is the Perry Monument in Cleveland—the first monument erected by that city. He also executed many portrait busts. He died in New York in 1895.

WELLSTEAD, J. G. (active 1844), Patentee—medallion bust of Theodore Freylinghuysen, 1844.

WHITFIELD, J. (active 1829–50), made portrait busts in New York and exhibited at the National Academy of Design.

WHITNEY, ANNE (1821–1915) was born in Watertown, Massachusetts. She was brought up in comfortable circumstances and at an early age turned her attention to writing poetry and modeling portraits. She received no special instruction in modeling though at some time she attended Dr. Rimmer's lectures on anatomy. In 1859 she published a volume of poems and the following year opened a studio in Watertown as a sculptor. She later spent four years in Europe, studying in Rome, Munich, and Paris. On her return to Boston she opened a studio there in 1872. Though she was at heart a reformer and a thinker in advance of her times, she made little effort to publicize her ideas. She was however a darling of the feminists and suffragists, a shining example of emancipated womanhood; Frances Willard called her "a Woman of the Century." Among her sculptured works are portraits of Harriet Martineau, Leif Ericsson, and a full length statue of Samuel Adams, now in the National Capitol. She died at the advanced age of ninety-four in Boston, the last living member of the First American School of Sculpture.

WILCOX, JOSEPH (active 1859), an exhibitor at the National Academy of Design, New York.

WILSON, MRS. ? (active c. 1840–1850) was born near Cooperstown, New York, where her infancy and youth were "very much shadowed by domestic suffering." Her father's loss "of a large competency" prompted the family to move west to Cincinnati; there Mrs. Wilson met and married Dr. Wilson. Her interest in sculpture was prompted by a visit to a sculptor's studio (possibly that of Hiram Powers). She immediately essayed a bust of her husband. "She worked with so much energy that sometimes she would faint away, and on one of these occasions he said, 'if you are not more moderate, I will throw that thing out of the window!' But it was finished and proved a perfect likeness, and she chiseled it in stone. It is in her parlor at Cincinnati, a most beautiful bust and an admirable likeness, and seems like a miracle, considering it was her first attempt . . . She has a family of children, and is a devoted mother. We think *stone* will have but little chance with these beings of flesh and blood, whose minds and hearts she is carefully *modelling*. Perhaps family cares may be the true secret why female sculptors are so rare; but we congratulate this lady; that she has the true perception of the beautiful, and feel quite sure that it will mitigate the suffering from delicate health, and scatter fragrant flowers and healing herbs in the sometimes rugged paths of duty."[13]

WILSON, J. H. (active 1855, Chesterfield, Illinois), Patentee—cast-iron monument, 1855.

WILSON, JOSEPH (active 1844–57), an exhibitor at the National Academy of Design, New York.

[13] From Hannah Farnham Lee, *Familiar Sketches of Sculpture and Sculptors* (1854).

3 · THE SUCCESSORS

SOME AMERICAN SCULPTORS BORN BETWEEN 1830 AND 1850

1830–1840

AKERS, CHARLES (1835–1906)

BAERER, HENRY (1837–1908); born Germany, came to the
United States 1854.

BARTLETT, TRUMAN H. (1835–1923).

BIDWELL, MARY H. (active 1879).

BISSELL, GEORGE EDWIN (1839–1920).

BROOKS, CAROLINE SHAWK (1840–?); active 1880, Cincinnati.

BROOME, ISAAC (1836–1922).

CALVERLY, CHARLES (1833–1922).

COBB, CYRUS (1834–1903).

COBB, DARIUS (1834–1919).

CONKEY, SAMUEL (1830–1904).

CONNELY, PIERCE FRANCIS (1840–?).

CONRADS, CARL H. (1839–?); born Germany, came to United
States 1860; active Hartford.

DRADDY, JOHN G. (1833–1904).

FRAZEE, O. (active 1867); son of John?

FREEMAN, FLORENCE (1836–76).

HASELTINE, JAMES HENRY (1833–1907).

HENRY, ALBERT P. (1836–72).

HINTON, MRS. HOWARD (1834–1921).

HOSMER, HARRIET GOODHUE (1830–1908).

LAUTZ, WILLIAM (1838–1915).

MANGER, HEINRICH (1833–?).

MASON, C. D. (1830–1915).

MEADE, LARKIN G. (1835–1910).

MILLS, THEODORE AUGUSTUS (1839–1916). Son of Clark.

MOFFITT, JOHN M. (1837–87), born England; New York.

MUNDY, JOHNSON M. (1832–?).

NEY, ELIZABETH (1833–1907); born Westphalia; died Austin,
Texas.

O'BRIEN, JOHN (1834–1904); born Ireland; died Galveston,
Texas.

PARK, RICHARD HENRY (1832–?); active Florence 1890.

POWERS, LONGWORTH (1835–1904); Florence. Son of Hiram
Powers.

REBISSO, LOUIS T. (1837–99); born Genoa.

RICKETSON, WALTON (1839–?); active 1925?

SIMMONS, FRANKLIN (1839–1913).

SMITH, CARL ROHL (?–1900).

SPRING, EDWARD ADOLPHUS (1837–?).

STRECKER, HERMAN (1836–1901).

THOMPSON, LAUNT (1833–94).

TURNER, WILLIAM GREEN (1833–1917).

VALENTINE, EDWARD V. (1838–1930).

WARD, JOHN QUINCY ADAMS (1830–1910).

1841–1850

CALDER, ALEXANDER MILNE (1846–1923).

CASELLAR, FERNANDO (1842–1925).

DUVENECK, FRANK (1848–1919).

ELLICOTT, HENRY JACKSON (1847–1901).

EZEKIEL, MOSES (1844–1917).

FRENCH, DANIEL CHESTER (1850–1931).

HARNISCH, ALBERT E. (1843–?).

HARTLEY, JONATHAN S. (1845–?).

HOXIE, MRS. (VINNIE REAM) (1847–1914).

KEMYS, EDWARD (1843–1907).

KEYSER, EPHRAIM (1850–?); active Baltimore 1934.

KITSON, SAMUEL JONES (1848–1906); born England; died
New York.

LEWIS, EDMONIA (1845–?).

MILLMORE, JOSEPH (1842–86).

MILLMORE, MARTIN (1845–83).

NEVIN, BLANCHE (1841–1925).

O'DONOVAN, WILLIAM R. (1844–1920).

PELL, ELLA FERRIS (1846–?); active 1934.

PERRY, JOHN D. (1845–?).

POPE, ALEXANDER (1849–1924).

POWERS, PRESTON (1843–?).

ROBERTS, HOWARD (1843–1900).

SAINT GAUDENS, AUGUSTUS (1848–1907).

WARNER, OLIN (1844–96).

WEIR, JOHN FERGUSON (1841–1926).

APPENDIX

EARLY NINETEENTH-CENTURY AMERICAN SCULPTURE IN THE COLLECTION OF THE METROPOLITAN MUSEUM OF ART

BALL, THOMAS (1819–1911). Bust of Daniel Webster, 1868.

BRACKETT, EDWARD AUGUSTUS (1818–1908). Bust of Washington Allston, c.1845.

BROWN, HENRY KIRKE (1814–86). Bust of Thomas Cole, c.1840; bust of Major General Philip Kearny, c.1865.

CLEVENGER, SHOBAL VAIL (1812–43). Bust of Henry Clay, c.1842.

CRAWFORD, THOMAS (1813–57). *Genius of Mirth*, 1843; *Mexican Princess*, 1848; *Babes in the Wood*, 1851.

GREENOUGH, RICHARD SALTONSTALL (1819–1904). *Circe*, 1853.

HUGHES, ROBERT BALL (1806–68). Bust of John Watts, c.1830.

HUNT, WILLIAM MORRIS (1824–79). *The Flight of Night*, c. 1847.

IVES, CHAUNCEY BRADLEY (1810–94). *Rebecca at the Well*, 1866.

MACDONALD, JAMES WILSON ALEXANDER (1824–1908). Bust of General Winfield Scott Hancock, c.1880.

MOZIER, JOSEPH (1812–70). *Rizpah*, 1869.

PALMER, ERASTUS DOW (1817–1904). *Indian Girl*, or, *The Dawn of Christianity*, 1856; *The White Captive*, 1859.

POWERS, HIRAM (1805–73). Bust of Andrew Jackson, 1835; *Fisher Boy*, 1844; *California*, 1858.

RIMMER, WILLIAM (1816–79). *The Falling Gladiator*, 1861; *The Dying Centaur*, 1871; *The Fighting Lions*, c.1870.

RINEHART, WILLIAM HENRY (1825–74). *Antigone*, 1870; *Clytie*, 1872; *Latona and Her Children, Apollo and Diana*, 1874.

ROGERS, JOHN (1829–1904). *"Wounded to the Rear," One More Shot*, 1865; *George Washington*, 1875.

ROGERS, RANDOLPH (1825–92). *Ruth*, c.1854; *Nydia*, 1859; *Indian Group, The Last Shot*, 1880.

SIMMONS, FRANKLIN (1839–1913). *The Promised Land*, 1874.

STORY, WILLIAM WETMORE (1819–95). *Medea*, 1868; *Cleopatra*, 1862; *Salome*, 1871.

VOLK, LEONARD WELLS (1828–95). Bust of Abraham Lincoln, 1860.

Anonymous. Bust of Henry Clay (miniature size), c.1830–1850; Statuette of Samuel F. B. Morse, c.1850–1880.

BIBLIOGRAPHY

Items on specific sculptors are listed under the sculptors' names.

Abbot, Jacob. Rollo's Tour in Europe: Rollo in Rome. Boston, 1858.

Adams, Mrs. Henry. Letters . . . Boston, 1936.

Agard, Walter R. The Greek Tradition in Sculpture. Baltimore, 1930.

AKERS, BENJAMIN PAUL

Miller, Roscoe R. "An American Sculptor of Note," *Americana,* XXVII (1933).

Tuckerman, H. T. "Two of Our Sculptors: B. P. Akers and E. S. Bartholomew," *Hours at Home* (April, 1866).

Usher, Leila. "Paul Akers," *New England Magazine* (1894).

American Art Annual, 1898–1941.

American Sculptors of the Nineteenth Century (N. Y. Public Library, Scrapbook).

Amis, M. N. Historical Raleigh. Raleigh, 1913.

Anonymous. "Sculpture in the United States," *Atlantic Monthly,* Vol. XXII (Nov., 1868).

—— "Sculpture of Cincinnati," *United States Magazine and Democratic Review,* VIII (1844), 247.

ANNABLE, GEORGE OLIVER

Chapin, Howard M. "George Annable, Sculptor," *Rhode Island Historical Society Collections,* XXII (1929).

Appleton's Cyclopedia of American Biography.

Armstrong, D. M. Day before Yesterday. New York, 1920.

Arnold, John Nelson. Art and Artists of Rhode Island. Providence, Rhode Island Citizens Historical Society, 1905.

Art Journal. London, 1839–70.

Artist's Fund Society, New York. Exhibition Catalogues, 1862–67.

Ashe, Samuel A. David Patton, Architect of the North Carolina Capitol. Raleigh, 1909. Bulletin No. 4, North Carolina Historical Commission.

BALL, THOMAS

Ball, Thomas. My Three Score Years and Ten. Boston, 1892.

Partridge, W. O. "Thomas Ball." *New England Magazine,* n.s. XII (1895).

BARBEE, WILLIAM

Cosmopolitan Art Journal, IV (1860).

BARTHOLOMEW, EDWARD SHEFFIELD

Crane, Susan. "Edward Sheffield Bartholomew," *Connecticut Quarterly,* II, (1896).

Tuckerman, H. T. "Two of Our Sculptors: B. P. Akers and E. S. Bartholomew," *Hours at Home* (April, 1866).

Beard, Charles, and Mary Beard. The Rise of American Civilization. New ed. New York, 1942.

Beard, Miriam. A History of the Business Man. New York, 1938.

Belknap, Henry W. Artists and Craftsmen of Essex County, Massachusetts. Salem, Essex Institute, 1927.

Benjamin, S. G. W. Art in America. New York, 1880.

Bolton, Ethel Stanwood. American Wax Portraits. Boston, 1929.

BRACKETT, EDWARD AUGUSTUS

Brackett, E. A. Twilight Hours; or, Leisure Moments of an Artist. Boston, 1845. (Poems.)

—— My House, Chips the Builder Threw Away. Boston, 1904. (Poems.)

Brooks, Van Wyck. The Flowering of New England. New York, 1938.

—— New England: Indian Summer. New York, 1940.

Brown, Glenn. History of the United States Capitol. 2 vols. Washington, 1900–1903.

BROWN, HENRY KIRKE

"Henry Kirke Brown," *Studio,* n.s. II, (1886).

"Three Artists," *Pocumtuck Valley Memorial Association (Deerfield),* History and Proceedings. VII, (1929).

Burnet, Mary Q. Art and Artists of Indiana. New York, 1921.

Bush, Douglas. Mythology and the Romantic Tradition in English Poetry. Cambridge, Mass., 1937.

Chase, George H., and C. R. Post. A History of Sculpture. New York (1924).

Cist, Charles. Cincinnati in 1841. Cincinnati, 1841.

Clark, Edna M. Ohio Art and Artists. Richmond, Va., 1932.

Clark, William J. Great American Sculptures. Philadelphia, 1877.

Clement, Clara E., and Laurence Hutton. Artists of the Nineteenth Century. Boston, 1879.

CLEVENGER, SHOBAL VAIL

"Clevenger," *United States Magazine and Democratic Review,* Vol. VIII (Feb., 1844).

Robinson, Victor. The Don Quixote of Psychiatry. New York, 1919. (a biography of S. V. Clevenger, *jr.*)

Tuckerman, H. T. Italian Sketchbook. New York, 1848.

Cochran, Thomas C., and William Miller. The Age of Enterprise. New York, 1942.

Conner, R. D. W. Canova's Statue of Washington. Raleigh, North Carolina Historical Commission, 1910.

Cooper, James Fenimore. Correspondence. New Haven, 1922.

Cosmopolitan Art Journal; a Record of Art Criticism, Art Intelligence, and Biography, and Repository of Belle-Lettres Literature. New York, 1856–60.

CRAWFORD, THOMAS

"Crawford and His Last Work," *Art Journal,* XVII (1855).

"Crawford and His Washington," *Cosmopolitan Art Journal,* I (1856), 46.

"Crawford and Ives," *Cosmopolitan Art Journal,* IV (1860).

Crosby, Nathan.   Annual Obituary Notices of Eminent Persons. Vol. I: 1857. Boston, 1858.

Eliot, S.   "Thomas Crawford," *American Quarterly Church Review and Ecclesiastical Register,* XI (April, 1858).

Greene, George W.   Biographical Studies. New York, 1860.

Hicks, Thomas.   Thomas Crawford; Career, Character and Works. New York, 1858.

—— Eulogy on Thomas Crawford. New York, 1865.

Hillard, George S.   "Eulogy on Thomas Crawford." *Atlantic Monthly,* XXIV (July, 1869).

Launitz, Robert E.   "Reminiscences of Thomas Crawford," *The Crayon,* VI (1859).

Osgood, Saumel.   Thomas Crawford and Art in America. New York, 1875.

Sumner, Charles.   "Thomas Crawford's Orpheus," *United States Magazine and Democratic Review,* XII (May, 1843).

"Thomas Crawford," *Art Journal,* XIX (1857). (Obit.)

"Thomas Crawford," *Cosmopolitan Art Journal,* II (1857).

"Thomas Crawford," *Living Age,* Ser. 2, XX (Jan.–March, 1858).

Tuckerman, Henry T.   "The Funeral of Thomas Crawford (poem)," *Cosmopolitan Art Journal,* II (1857–58).

Crayon, The; a Journal Devoted to the Graphic Arts. New York 1855–60.

DEXTER, HENRY

Albee, John.   Henry Dexter. Boston, 1898.

Dictionary of American Biography.

Dow, George Francis.   Arts and Crafts in New England, 1704–1775. Topsfield, 1927.

Dunlap, William.   History of the Rise and Progress of the Arts of Design in the United States. New York, 1834.

Durand, John.   The Life and Times of A. B. Durand. New York, 1894.

Ellet, Mrs. E. F.   Women Artists in All Ages and Countries. London, 1858.

Elliot, Frances.   Roman Gossip. London, 1896.

Elliott, Maude Howe.   Uncle Sam Ward and His Circle. New York, 1938.

Emerson, Ralph Waldo.   Essays; First Series, Second Series. New ed. Boston, 1885.

—— Journals; with annotations. Boston, 1909.

—— English Traits. Boston, 1881.

—— The Complete Essays and Other Writings of Ralph Waldo Emerson. Modern Library edition. New York, 1940.

Fairman, Charles E.   Art and Artists of the Capitol. Washington, 1927.

Fielding, Mantle.   Dictionary of American Painters, Sculptors, and Engravers. Philadelphia [1926].

Forbes, Harriette M.   "Early Portrait Sculpture in New England," *Old Time New England,* XIX (July, 1928).

Forrer, L.   Biographical Dictionary of Medalists. 8 vols. London, 1904–30.

Freeman, James E.   Gatherings from an Artist's Portfolio. Vol. I (New York, 1877); Vol. II (Boston, 1883).

French, H. W.   Art and Artists of Connecticut. Boston, 1879.

GARLICK, THEODATUS

Kelly, H. A., and W. L. Burrage.   American Medical Biographies. Baltimore, 1920.

Gottesman, R. S.   Arts and Crafts in New York, 1726–1776. New York, 1938.

Gould, W. M.   Zephyrs from Italy and Sicily. New York, 1852.

GREENOUGH, HORATIO

"Etchings with a Chisel," *United States Magazine and Democratic Review* (Feb., 1846).

Everett, Alexander.   "Greenough's Statue of Washington," *United States Magazine and Democratic Review* (June, 1844).

Greenough, Frances B.   Letters of Horatio Greenough. Boston, 1887.

Greenough, Horatio.   The Travels, Observations, and Experiences of a Yankee Stonecutter, by Horace Bender (pseud.). New York, 1852.

N., B. J.   "Horatio Greenough," *Knickerbocker Magazine* (April, 1836).

Salisbury, Edward S.   "Two letters of Horatio Greenough," *Magazine of American History* (Oct., 1887).

Spiller, Robert E.   "Fenimore Cooper, Critic of His Times: New Letters from Rome and Paris, 1830–31," *American Literature,* Vol. 1, No. 2 (May, 1929).

—— Fenimore Cooper, Critic of His Times. New York, 1931.

Tuckerman, H. T.   A Memorial of Horatio Greenough. New York, 1853.

Greve, Charles.   Centennial History of Cincinnati. Chicago, 1904.

Hart, Charles Henry.   "Unknown Life Masks of Great Americans," *McClures Magazine,* IX (1897).

—— "Life Masks of Great Americans," *McClures Magazine,* XII (1898–99).

HART, JOEL TANNER

Biographical Encyclopedia of Kentucky. Cincinnati, 1878.

Breckinridge, Issa Desha   "The Work Shall Praise the Master," a Memorial to Joel T. Hart, the Kentucky Sculptor, from the Women of the Blue Grass. Cincinnati, 1884.

Warfield, Ethelbert Dudley.   "Joel T. Hart, the Kentucky Sculptor," *Magazine of Western History,* II (1885).

Hawthorne, Nathaniel.   The Marble Faun. First published 1860.

—— Passages from the French and Italian Note-Books. Boston, 1899.

Hillard, George S.   Six Months in Italy. Boston, 1853.

HOSMER, HARRIET GOODHUE

Bradford, R. A. "Life and Works of Harriet Hosmer," *New England Magazine*, n.s., XLV, 1911.

Carr, Cornelia. Harriet Hosmer, Letters and Memories. New York, 1912.

Howe, Henry. Memoirs of the Most Eminent American Mechanics. New York, 1858.

Howe, M. A. DeWolf. Memories of a Hostess (Mrs. J. T. Fields). Boston [1922].

Howe, Winifred E. A History of the Metropolitan Museum of Art. New York, 1913.

HUGHES, ROBERT BALL

Bolton, Ethel Stanwood. American Wax Portraits. Boston, 1929.

Orcutt, William D. Good Old Dorchester, a Narrative History of the Town, 1630–1893. Cambridge, 1893.

Hughes, Mrs. Robert Ball. MS letter (Metropolitan Museum of Art Library).

IVES, CHAUNCEY BRADLEY

Catalogue of Important Sculptures by the Late C. B. Ives ... 1899. American Art Galleries. New York.

"Crawford and Ives," *Cosmopolitan Art Journal*, IV (1860).

James, Henry. Roderick Hudson. Boston, 1917. (See under Story, W. W.)

Jarves, James Jackson. Art Hints. New York, 1855.

—— The Art Idea. New York, 1864.

—— Art Thoughts. New York, 1869.

—— Italian Rambles. New York, 1885.

JONES, THOMAS D.

Memories of Lincoln by Thomas D. Jones and Reproductions of the Author's Two Busts of Lincoln. New York, 1934. (Reprint from the *Sacramento Weekly Union*, Nov. 4, 1871.)

Kelby, William. Notes on American Artists, 1754–1820. New York, 1922.

Kimball, Fiske. Beginnings of Sculpture in Colonial America," *Art and Archaeology*, VIII (1919).

LANDER, LOUISA. "Miss Louisa Lander's Work," *Cosmopolitan Art Journal*, Vol. IV, No. 1 (1860).

Landor, Walter Savage. Landor's letter to Emerson. Cleveland, 1895.

Language of the Flowers ... by the Editor of "Forget Me Not," 4th American ed. Philadelphia, 1838.

Larrabee, Stephen A. English Bards and Grecian Marbles. New York, 1943.

Launitz, Robert E. "Reminiscences of Thomas Crawford," *The Crayon*, VI (1859).

Lee, Hannah Farnham. Familiar Sketches of Sculpture and Sculptors. Boston, 1854.

Lenox Library. Guide to the Paintings and Sculptures Exhibited to the Public. New York, 1880.

Lester, Charles Edwards. The Artists of America. New York, 1846.

—— My Consulship. New York, 1853.
(See under Powers, Hiram)

MACDONALD, JAMES WILSON ALEXANDER

Clark, Edna M. Ohio Art and Artists. Richmond, Va., 1932.

Marceau, Henri. William Rush, 1756–1833, the First Native American Sculptor. Philadelphia, 1937.

Marquand, Allan, and A. L. Frothingham. Text Book of the History of Sculpture. New York, 1899.

Matthews, T. The Biography of John Gibson, R.A., Sculptor, Rome. London, 1911.

Mayer, Frank B. With Pen and Pencil on the Frontier in 1851. St. Paul, Minn., 1932.

Mechlin, Leila. "Art Life in Washington," *Records of the Columbia Historical Society*. Washington, D. C., XXIV (1922).

Metropolitan Museum of Art. Bulletin. 1906–date.

—— Catalogue of Sculpture, 1741–1907.

—— Clipping Files.

—— Secretary's Files.

MILLS, CLARK

"American Arts and American Arms," *Graham's Magazine* (Jan., 1854).

Mills, Clark. An Address before the Jefferson Democratic Association of the First District at Holland's Store. Washington, D. C., 1877.

Bocock, Thomas S. Inauguration of the Mills statue of George Washington, 1860. Oration by T. S. Bocock; An Address by the artist, Clark Mills.

Hart, William Octave. "Clark Mills," *Records of the Columbia Historical Society*, XXIV (1922).

Rutledge, Anna Wells. "Cogdell and Mills, Charleston Sculptors," *Antiques*, XLI (March, 1942).

Morse, Edward Lind. Samuel F. B. Morse; His Letters and Journals. Boston, 1914.

MOZIER, JOSEPH

Osgood, Samuel. "American Artists in Italy," *Harpers Magazine* (Aug., 1870).

Photographs of the Work of Joseph Mozier (a portfolio of 27 photographs in the New York Public Library).

Scheirr, Rodman. "Joseph Mozier and His Handiwork," *Potter's American Monthly* (Jan., 1876).

Mumford, Lewis. Technics and Civilization. New York, 1934.

National Academy of Design. Catalogues of Annual Exhibitions, 1831–66.

National Cyclopedia of American Biography.

New York American, Monday, June 27th, 1831 (report of fire in state capitol, Raleigh, N. C.).

New York City. Catalogue of Works of Art Belonging to the City of New York, 1909–1920.

New York Historical Society. Catalogue of American Portraits. New York, 1941.

New York Historical Society. National Academy of Design Exhibition Record 1826–1860. (Bartlett Cowdray, Comp.) New York, 1943.

Noble, Louis L. The Course of Empire . . . and Other Pictures of Thomas Cole. New York, 1853.

PALMER, ERASTUS DOW. The Philosophy of the Ideal. Albany, 1856.

—— The Palmer Marbles. Albany, 1856.

—— Ingham, Charles. "Erastus Dow Palmer; a Great American Sculptor," *American Historical Magazine,* XXIV (1930).

Parrington, Vernon L. Main Currents in American Thought. New York, 1930.

Paris. Exposition Universelle, 1855. Notes of Some Remarkable Objects Exhibited in the . . . Paris Universal Exhibition. London, 1855.

Partridge, William O. "The American School of Sculpture," *Arena,* VII (1892–93).

Peabody, Elizabeth (editor). Aesthetic Papers. Boston, 1849. Article I, "Criticism" by Samuel G. Ward.

Philadelphia. The Stranger's Guide in Philadelphia. Philadelphia, 1860.

Pierce, Edward L. Memoir and Letters of Charles Sumner. Boston, 1878.

Pinckney, Pauline A. American Figureheads and Their Carvers. New York, 1940.

POWERS, HIRAM

Atlee, Y. S. "Hiram Powers," *Living Age,* XLII (1854), 569.

Bellows, H. W. "Seven Sittings with Powers the Sculptor," *Appleton's Journal,* I (1869).

Boynton, Henry. "Hiram Powers," *New England Magazine,* n. s., Vol. 20, No. 5 (July, 1899).

Chambrun, Clara. The Making of Nicholas Longworth. New York, 1933.

Cincinnati Museum of Art. Exhibition of Paintings by Joseph Oriel Eaton and Sculpture by Hiram Powers. Cincinnati, 1934.

Connolly, Louise. Hiram Powers, the Sculptor. Newark, N. J., Newark Museum, 1926.

Everett, Edward. A Defense of Powers' Statue of Webster. Boston, 1859.

—— "Hiram Powers the Sculptor," *Living Age,* XV (1847).

Hawthorne, Nathaniel. "The Studio of Hiram Powers," *Every Saturday,* XI (1871).

Jarves, J. J. "Hiram Powers," *Art Journal,* n.s., XIII (1874).

Kellogg, Miner K. Justice to Hiram Powers. Cincinnati, 1848.

—— Mr. Miner K. Kellogg to his friends. Paris, 1858.

Lester, Charles Edwards. The Artist, the Merchant, and

the Statesman of the Age of the Medici and of Our Own Time. New York, 1845.

—— "The Genius and Sculpture of Hiram Powers," *American Whig Review,* II (1845).

Lewis, Anna. "Art and Artists of America: Hiram Powers," *Graham's Magazine,* XLVIII (Nov., 1855).

Powers, E. L. "Reminiscences of My Father," *Vermonter,* Feb.–March, 1907.

Powers, Hiram. "Letters of Hiram Powers to Nicholas Longworth," *Historical and Philosophical Society of Ohio, Quarterly Publication,* I (1906).

Robinson, C. S. "A Morning with Hiram Powers," *Hours at Home,* VI (1867).

T., B. B. (Thacher). "Sketch of a Selfmade Sculptor," *Knickerbocker Magazine* (April, 1835).

Prezzolini, Giuseppe. Come gli americani scoprirono l'Italia, 1750–1850. Milano, 1933.

(Chap. VIII, "Gli artisti americani in Italia.")

Price, S. W. Old Masters of the Blue Grass. Louisville, Ky., 1902.

Prime, Alfred Cox. Arts and Crafts in Philadelphia, Maryland, and South Carolina. 2 vols. Topsfield, 1929–32.

Proske, Beatrice Gilman. Brookgreen Gardens, Sculpture. Brookgreen, S. C., 1943.

Radcliffe, Alida G. Schools and Masters of Sculpture. New York, 1894.

RIMMER, WILLIAM

American Art Review, I (Boston, 1880).

Architectural Record, XXI (1907).

Bartlett, Truman H. The Art Life of William Rimmer. Boston, 1882. (Reviewed in *Atlantic Monthly,* Feb., 1883.)

—— "William Rimmer," in *American Art and American Art Collections.* Boston, 1889.

Borglum, Gutzon. "Our Prophet Unhonored in Art," *New York Evening Post,* June 18, 1921.

Metropolitan Museum of Art. *Bulletin,* I (May, 1906), 91; II (Nov., 1907), 188.

RINEHART, WILLIAM HENRY

Rusk, William Sener. William Henry Rinehart, Sculptor. Baltimore, 1939. (Contains an exhaustive bibliography.)

ROGERS, JOHN

Eaton. "Catching up with John Rogers," *Magazine of Art,* XI (Sept., 1920).

Groups of Statuary by John Rogers. New York, 1875 (Catalogue).

Ibid. New York, 1877 (Catalogue).

LaFollette, S. in *Art in America.* New York, 1929.

New York Historical Society Quarterly Bulletin, XVI (April, 1932–Jan., 1933).

Partridge, W. O. John Rogers, the People's Sculptor," *New England Magazine,* n.s., XIII (Feb., 1896).

Smith, Chetwood. Rogers Groups, Thought and Wrought by John Rogers. Boston, 1934.

ROGERS, RANDOLPH

D'Ooge, Martin. Catalogue of the Gallery of Art and Archaeology of the University of Michigan. Ann Arbor, 1892.

Rourke, Constance. Roots of American Culture. New York [1942].

Samek, Sergio. "Bibliografia di viaggiatori straniere in Italia nel secolo XIX," *Annales Institutorum ... Romae,* 1935–39, Vols. 7, 8, 9–10.

Shoemaker, William D. Patents for Designs. Washington, 1929.

SIMMONS, FRANKLIN

Whiting, Lilian. "A Veteran Sculptor," *Outlook,* XCVIII (May 27, 1911).

STEBBINS, EMMA. Charlotte Cushman: Her Letters and Memories of Her Life. Boston, 1879.

STONE, HORATIO. Freedom. Washington, 1864 (Poem).

STORY, WILLIAM WETMORE

"American Artists and American Art, Pt. V: William Wetmore Story," *American Magazine of Art,* II (1879).

James, Henry. William Wetmore Story and His Friends. Boston, 1903.

Phillips, M. E. Reminiscences of William Wetmore Story. Chicago, 1897.

"Romance of Beautiful American Marchese Peruzzi di Medici Daughter of Sculptor Story," *New York Sun* (Sunday, April 27, 1913).

Story, W. W. Conversations in a Studio. Boston, 1890.

—— Graffitti d'Italia. New York, 1868.

—— Proportions of the Human Figure. London, 1866.

—— Excursions in Art and Literature. Boston, 1891.

Wallace, Mrs. Lew. "William Wetmore Story; a Memory," *Cosmopolitan Magazine,* XXI (Sept., 1896).

Swain, David L. Early Times in Raleigh. Raleigh, 1867.

Swann, Mabel M. The Athenaeum Gallery, 1827–1873. Boston, 1840.

Sumner, Charles. The Scholar, the Jurist, the Artist, the Philanthropist. Mr. Sumner's address before the Phi Beta Kappa Society ... Harvard. Boston, 1846.

Taft, Lorado. The History of American Sculpture. New York, 1930.

Trollope, Frances. A Visit to Italy. London, 1842.

—— Domestic Manners of the Americans. London, 1832.

Trollope, T. A. What I Remember. London, 1887.

Tuckerman, H. T. Leaves from the Diary of a Dreamer. London, 1853.

—— The Book of the Artists. New York, 1869.

—— Italian Sketchbook. New York, 1848.

Twain, Mark. Innocents Abroad. Hartford, 1901.

United States Patent Office. An Account of the Destruction by Fire ... of the Model Room ... 1877. Washington, 1877.

—— List of Patents for Inventions and Designs, Issued by the United States, from 1790 to 1847. Washington, 1847.

—— Reports of the Commissioner of Patents, 1847–70.

VOLK, LEONARD WELLS

Biographical Sketches of the Leading Men of Chicago. Chicago, 1868.

Volk, Leonard Wells. "The Lincoln Life Mask and How It Was Made," *The Century,* XXIII (Dec., 1881).

Walter, Cornelia. "Mount Auburn," in *Rural Cemeteries of America.* New York, 1847.

Ward, Artemus. Artemus Ward: His Works, Complete. New York, 1875.

Waters, Asa. Thomas Blanchard and His Inventions. Worcester, 1878.

Whiting, Lilian. The Florence of Landor. Boston, 1905.

WHITNEY, ANNE

Spofford, Harriet. A Little Book of Friends. Boston, 1916.

Whitney, Anne. Poems. New York, 1859.

Willard, Frances E., and M. L. Livermore. A Woman of the Century. Buffalo, 1893.

PLATES

FIG. I. STATUARY ROOM OF THE ATHENAEUM, BOSTON (1850-1860)

FIG. 2. STUDIO OF HIRAM POWERS, FLORENCE (1850-1860)

FIG. 1. POWERS'S GREEK SLAVE
AT THE DÜSSELDORF GALLERY, NEW YORK (1857)

FIG. 2. TOURISTS IN THE GALLERIES OF THE VATICAN
(1858)

FIG. 3. ITALIAN IMAGE-MAKERS, NEW YORK (1850-1860)

GEORGE WASHINGTON BY HORATIO GREENOUGH, 1832-1843

ANDREW JACKSON BY HIRAM POWERS, 1836-1837

FIG. 1. THE GENIUS OF MIRTH BY THOMAS CRAWFORD
1843

FIG. 2. THE WHITE CAPTIVE BY ERASTUS DOW PALMER
1859

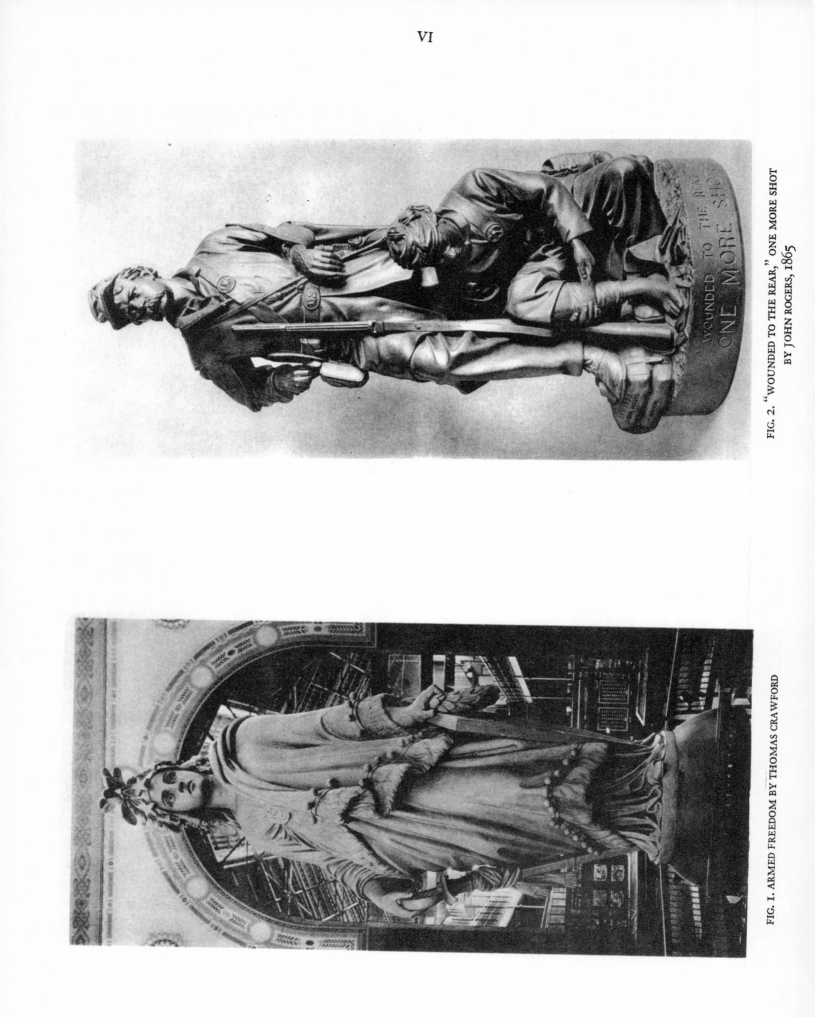

FIG. 2. "WOUNDED TO THE REAR," ONE MORE SHOT
BY JOHN ROGERS, 1865

FIG. I. ARMED FREEDOM BY THOMAS CRAWFORD

FIG. 2. HENRY CLAY BY SHOBAL VAIL CLEVENGER, 1842

FIG. 1. WASHINGTON ALLSTON BY EDWARD AUGUSTUS BRACKETT, 1844

FIG. 1. CLEOPATRA BY WILLIAM WETMORE STORY, 1858

FIG. 2. LATONA AND HER CHILDREN BY WILLIAM HENRY RINEHART, 1873-1874

THE DYING CENTAUR BY WILLIAM RIMMER, C. 1870

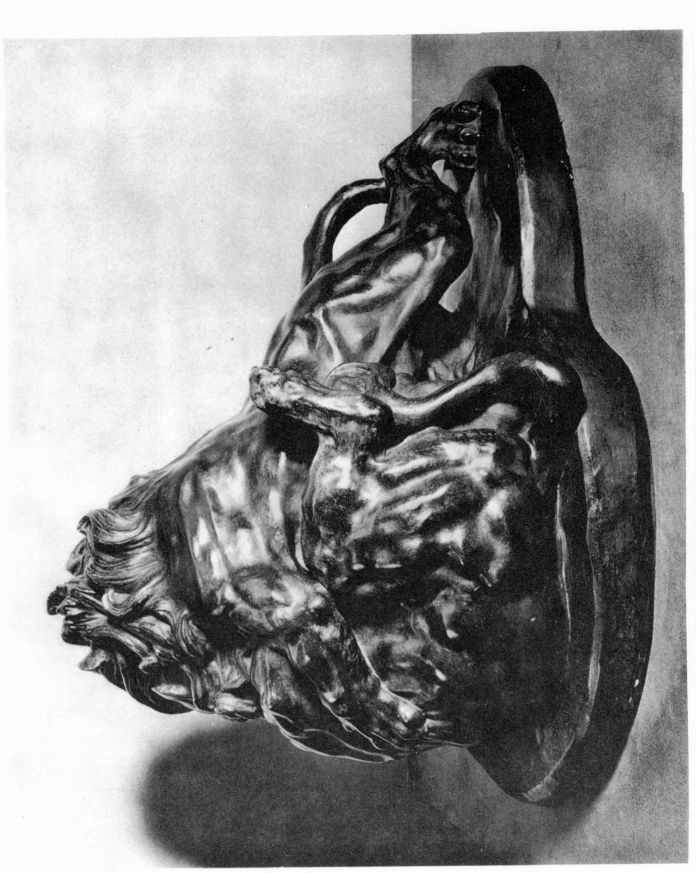

THE FIGHTING LIONS BY WILLIAM RIMMER, C. 1870

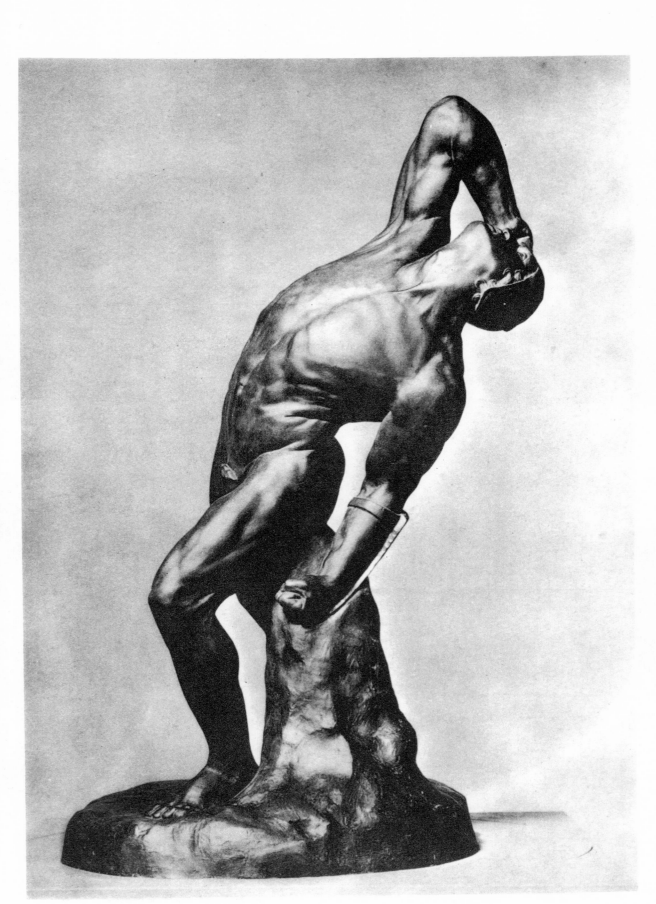

THE FALLING GLADIATOR BY WILLIAM RIMMER, C. 1861

FIG. I. ANDREW JACKSON MONUMENT BY CLARK MILLS, 1853

FIG. 2. VIEW IN THE SCULPTURE GALLERY, METROPOLITAN MUSEUM OF ART, NEW YORK (1890-1900)

INDEX